# RELEASE YOUR FAITH

## ACHIEVE THE GOALS THROUGH THE BREAKTHROUGH OF FAITH

DR. HELIO V. NESPOLI

# RELEASE YOUR FAITH

## ACHIEVE THE GOALS THROUGH THE BREAKTHROUGH OF FAITH

DR. HELIO V. NESPOLI

**RELEASE YOUR FAITH**
ACHIEVE THE GOALS THROUGH
THE BREAKTHROUGH OF FAITH

Dr. Helio V. Nespoli

First Edition | August 2023

**COVER:** Helio V. Nespoli
**LAYOUT:** Ligia Marquardt Pesch

Publishing by **Releaseyourfaith.org**
https://releaseyourfaith.org/

This book is written to provide information and motivation to readers. Its purpose is not to render any type of psychological, legal, or professional advice of any kind. The content is the sole opinion and expression of the author.

All scripture quotations and verses used in this book are taken from the Scripture taken from the Holy Bible, NEW INTERNATIONAL VERSION®, NIV® Copyright © 1973, 1978, 1984, 2011 by Biblica, Inc.® Used by permission. All rights reserved worldwide, according to https://www.biblica.com/terms-of-use.

Printed in the United States of America

**ISBN: 979-8-218-95807-7 (Paperback)**

Library of Congress Catalogue-in-Publication Data

Names: Nespoli, Helio, author

Title: Release your faith

# CONTENTS

# DEDICATION

I want to dedicate this book to the thousands of people who have responded positively to the message contained in this book throughout my ministry, in the churches, seminars, encounters, speeches, and individually, which brought me the joy of seeing accomplished in their lives the reason why I was born: to serve people.

I also want to dedicate this book to my beloved wife, Silvia Nespoli, who has been an inspiration, an example, and a blessing in my life. She has been a blessing not just to me and our family, but also to all the thousands of people she has been in contact with and also has counseled and ministered to. Been sensitive to the Lord to inspire her every weekday since 2014, with a 5-minute message in Portuguese (posted on WhatsApp, Instagram, Facebook, and YouTube), and also in English (starting in May/2023), reaching people in several places and different Countries, displays a true work of faith, and it demonstrates her heart and the call we both share, which is to serve people.

Silvia, I love you forever!

# ENDORSEMENTS

Faith is not a mental effort to think positively. The origin of true faith is always God, so faith is relational. It is when we are so committed to God that He speaks to us, and we respond by acting up to what He has spoken and directed us. Faith makes us co-creators with God and true agents of His will. This book will surely take you to a new dimension of life and purpose. Enter this reading with sensitivity and expectation.

**Pr. Marcos de Souza Borges (Coty)**
*International speaker, missionary since 1986 at YWAM (Youth With A Mission), where he is a director in Brazil, and author of 16 books, where one of them is a best seller (Intelligent Shepherding), founder and creator of EIFOL (Integral School for training of Deliverers), a seminar that has impacted and trained thousands of leaders in Brazil and internationally in the inner healing and deliverance ministry.*

# BACKGROUND

Born in an evangelical home in 1959, Hélio Vassão Nespoli had a real encounter with the Lord Jesus at age 15, on 11/01/1974.

He has been married to Silvia Nespoli since 1982, with whom he has 3 adult children. He was ordained pastor of the gospel in 1985 and founded and pastored 7 churches both in Brazil and the USA. He had a secular job as an animal dentist, specialized in large animals, from 1981 through 1997, mainly treating horses and correcting their bites with braces in Brazil and later in 25 States of the USA. In 1997, he was accredited by the State of Florida as a "business broker" (professional specializing in the sales of companies). He brought American multimillion Dollar's investments to Brazil (including Harvard University's endowment fund and Prudential Insurance Company). Dr Nespoli attended the former Florida Theological Seminary in Orlando, Florida (currently known as the Florida Christian University), where he received his Bachelor's, master's, and Doctorate degrees in Biblical studies, and where he also taught both in Portuguese and English at the time when Dr. Harold L. Shindoll was its president. In 1997 his wife was ordained a pastor and, along with Dr Nespoli, founded the Brazilian Ministers Alliance of Central Florida, uniting the Brazilian ministers of Orlando and the region. In 2012, Pastor Helio also created the REDIMA Seminar (REsgatando a DIgnidade MAsculina – Redeeming the Male Dignity), where he ministers to men about returning to the original principles of God and how to attain God's purpose for their lives. At the same time, his wife, Pastor Silvia, ministers the REVIVA to the women (REcuperando uma VIda de VAlor – Restoring a Worthy Life), addressing the various challenges women face and how to live life satisfied in God. As a couple, Pastors Helio and Silvia also minister a seminar entitled IN LOVE I and II for couples both in churches of various denominations as well as in other organizations, where the spiritual and relational bases that God created for the couple and the home are ministered by both pastors. With matrimonial experience since 1982, plus the 5-1/2 years of courtship, there is an experience and journey with God that they share with couples. Pastors Helio and Silvia were appointed counselors at EIFOL (an associated ministry of YWAM – Youth with a Mission), the couple resides in the Dallas area, Texas, in the USA.

Throughout his life, Dr. Nespoli has exercised and lived by faith. After understanding how faith works, which is explained in this book, he was able to fulfill the calling of

God to his life, which is to help people to achieve their full potential in God and accomplish the purpose why they were born.

This book is not just theory, but the expression of a reality the author has practiced and the victories he was able to achieve, by breaking the shell of the seed of faith, enabling it to be released and bear fruits in and through his life for the glory of God.

FAITH WORKS!!!

# INTRODUCTION

There is a way to activate your faith through new actions that will enable you to achieve all that God has for you to reach.

Did you ever feel that there is more to accomplish in your life that, for some reason, you were not able to achieve? Do you see other people conquering, advancing, and moving forward, while you see that there is something "blocking" you to move forward and to reach the same results in your life? Do you see that you have come to stagnation in your walk or in one area of your life that all the efforts you have made couldn't make it change or improve at all?

This book has not come to you just by coincidence or by chance... there is a reason you are having the opportunity to read it. I am sure it will be able to answer so many questions you have and solve so many problems you are or even will face in your life! You will be able to identify the area that is blocked and the reason why it is blocked, so you will be able to face it and break that resistance and see the fruits and results of this breakthrough!

Several years ago, I received a revelation about faith, and how to activate it that has changed my life and I want to share this revelation with you, so you too will know how faith works, how it can be activated, and your goals be reached. Don't take it for granted, as this book contains very precious information that took me decades and countless hours of meditation, studying, reading, and praying to be able to share with you.

This is the revelation:

Jesus has mentioned in Mathew 17:20:

> *"And He said to them, "Because of your little faith. For truly I say to you, if you have faith as of a mustard seed, you will say to this mountain, 'Move from here to there,' and it will move. And nothing will be impossible for you." Berean Literal Bible*

The word for "as of" in the original is: "hós", which means: as, like as, about, as it were, and according as. So, Jesus is declaring that faith is like a seed.

A seed is a grain that consists of three elements: core/nucleus, cotyledon/endosperm, and shell/seed coat.

All the DNA, genetic material, and information are lodged in the core, the nucleus, which must be released for the multiplying property of the seed to germinate and produce.

Most of us had the experience in elementary school when we placed a pinto bean on the wet cotton as we were learning how the germination process works. Did you have it? Do you remember it?

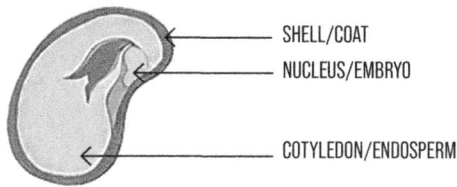

The first thing that has happened was the shell of the bean dying and shrinking, releasing the inner part, the nucleus, that started coming out and reaching the wet cotton to form a new plant. It was the breakthrough of the seed to germinate and produce.

This is the breakthrough that Jesus mentioned in John 12:23,24, when he spoke about his own death:

> *"The hour has come that the Son of Man should be glorified. Truly, truly, I say to you, unless a grain of wheat falls into the earth and dies, it remains alone; but if it dies, it bears much fruit".*

Just like us, Jesus was tripartite, he was formed in three parts: spirit, soul, and body. In this verse, He is saying that if the grain does not die, it remains alone. What did die when Jesus was on the cross? His spirit, His soul, or His body? Of course, it was His body, the shell, so the soul and the spirit (the inner parts) were released!

We can bring the same analogy to faith as a seed, so the outer part, the shell, must die to release the inner part. According to Jesus, if it does not die, it stays alone, without producing what it should be producing, hindering the powerful DNA that is lodged inside the nucleus, making it unfruitful.

The apostle Paul also declares that the seed must die in order to live, in 1 Corinthians 15:36b:

> "... When you put a seed into the ground, it doesn't grow into a plant unless it dies first."

By this understanding, we start to unveil the revelation that, for our faith to be productive, the shell, which is the outer layer must die.

In the next chapters we will go through 16 potential "shells", or "parts of the shell" that may be blocking your faith, making its tremendous and powerful genetic material to be hidden, locked, unfruitful and unproductive.

You will be able to identify the shells or the parts of the shell that must be broken, and this breakthrough will enable you to achieve all the accomplishments and conquests that you could and even should be reaching.

The definition of faith, according to Hebrew 11:1 is:

> "Now faith is confidence in what we hope for and assurance about what we do not see".

Faith is not just a strong desire, but an assurance of what we do not see, which means that we have an inner certainty about it, even without seeing the physical evidence of it.

We still need faith to do something, even if we already have all the provisions for it and have traced and mitigated every single risk that decision requires.

There is always an unknown factor in every area of life, and this is why faith is the base because we are very limited on knowing the future and all the factors that are involving a situation. For instance, we can't read the minds, intentions, and reactions of the people involved directly or indirectly in the situation, and predict all the external factors, like political changes, climate, dangers, catastrophes, laws, regulations, unknown factors, etc., etc., etc.

This demonstrates how much faith is an essential part of our lives and must be practiced every single day in every area.

A "leap of faith" is when we don't have all the facts and the consequences already lined up and figured out but move forward anyway.

Faith is the basic element, granted by the Creator, that enables us to keep on moving and living.

There is the basic faith, which is something every human being has received from God, according to Romans 12:3b: *"...as God has given to each one a measure of faith"*. This is the faith that makes people raise up every morning, go to work or school, raising a family, pursue a career, sowing, harvesting, etc. This is the basic faith, which is the belief system that every human being was born with.

There is also a supernatural faith that is given when someone uses the basic faith to believe in the Lord Jesus Christ, and accept him as their personal savior. This is a faith for salvation. This is why the Bible mentions in 2 Thessalonians 3:2: *"and that we may be delivered from perverse and evil men; for not everyone is of the faith"* (BLB). The word "faith" in this verse is "pistis", which is referring to the supernatural faith, which evil and perverse men don't have.

According to what Jesus said in Matthew 17:20, faith is like a seed. Faith is very powerful and carries the DNA of multiplication.

What is a seed? It is something that carries all the characteristics of what has generated it, and the power to multiply those characteristics. This multiplying characteristic of the seed is like this: when we see an orange tree full of oranges; we can count all the seeds that are in each orange, but we can't calculate the number of orange trees that will produce several oranges each little seed has the power to produce. This means that, through the power of faith, not only our lives can see multiplication, but we can also leave a legacy of accomplishments (spirit, soul, and body) that will impact future generations.

My intention with this book is to stir up all the power that this faith that you have inside of you, given by God to produce, to make you move, to advance, to conquer, and most important: to find and fulfill the purpose for that you have been born to fulfill.

The Bible tells us about two kinds of faith, according to James 2:14 to 24: living and dead faith. The living faith produces works, and the dead faith produces nothing. The living faith is displayed by actions, works, deeds, etc. Actually, we must **live** by faith, according to Galatians 3:11, which means that we don't only "use" faith for a special moment or situation; it is as important as the oxygen we need to live.

As an example, I want to share with you experiences that I personally had in my life using this understanding and revelation, that made me accomplish things that only by faith could be reached. I will also share testimonies of others and some biblical ones.

First example: when I was 22 years of age there was no Internet, no cell phones, not even computers... the year was 1981. I was enrolled and studying at Methodist University in one special buco-maxillo-facial prosthetic course at the Human Dentistry Department. I've always had a passion for the country, farms, and large animals, like cows and horses. Someone showed me an article in a newspaper about cows' teeth being treated in Argentina and Uruguay with the name of the technician that was doing it. After meeting with the professor at the veterinarian school of the largest University in Brazil, I understood that no one was fixing cow's teeth in Brazil and there was a gap to be fulfilled in this area. By faith, and the support of the President of the Methodist University, I went from Brazil to Argentina and Uruguay by bus to check out and learn how that professional was treating cows' teeth, of whom I only had a name. I didn't learn to speak Spanish, which is the language they speak in those two countries, but by faith I was able to communicate somehow (consulting the public phone books and going to universities to get information) and, after reaching some dead ends, I've found the person that was doing it and got all the information I needed to enable me to introduce bulls and cow's teeth treatment in Brazil. How, at a very young age, was I able to convince Brazilian farmers and cattle breeders that were breeding for a long time, that their animals could have teeth problems? Only by understanding how faith works and pursuing the goal with all my strength, even after all the criticism, skepticism, and hundreds of huge "NOS" from the breeders I've entered in contact with. After a while, I was treating large animals all over the country for the most known breeders of cattle and horses and, after moving to the USA, working with horses, serving 288 horse breeders and trainers in 25 States, even developing braces to correct horse's bite without the help of any book or literature, only by praying and believing... faith works!

After moving to the US, the biggest hurdle that really challenged my faith, was understanding what some breeders and trainers were saying on the phone, with the country accent they had, mainly giving me directions to their farms and ranches, not being able to see their lips, but thank God I was able to understand... faith works!

There will be more testimonies of challenges and situations I've encountered in my life that I intend to share during this book, that I sincerely hope to help you to keep on believing... I will not be sharing to brag, but just as a testimony of real experiences that a regular guy like me was able to overcome and hopefully will help and encourage you to overcome whatever situations you are or will be facing...

FAITH WORKS!!!!

# CHAPTER 1

# OPPOSING ARGUMENTS
## (Reasoning)

O ur minds work with logic. Our brains are always trying to find a way to save energy by not thinking too hard about something, so, if it doesn't make sense, it just doesn't spend energy with it, by saying to itself: "Let's just forget it! It is not going to happen, period!" So, it shuts down to accepting that what you are looking for will be accomplished.

This is the part of the shell where the mind tries to "understand" or "rationalize" what faith is trying to produce, creating conflicting thoughts; the mind dominates, does not accept, and does not submit to simply receiving something that it cannot control or understand. The memories of bad experiences block faith, arguing with itself, saying: "How is this supposed to happen"? "This makes no sense, it is very complicated, this is impossible to happen".

Here are some practical examples of thoughts that "attack" our faith, making the shell harder to break and the power of faith to be released, that would be able to change the situation completely:

- The doctor gives you a certain diagnosis and there is no treatment to cure it, so your thoughts of desperation start to flood your mind:

- You think: *"I am a failure... there is no hope for me... I believe the only way is for me to kill myself and end up my life, so this pain will finally stop"*;

- The bank manager says there is nothing that can be done financially for your case, and they will have to foreclose the property;

- The spouse says to you that there is no more hope for the marriage, that divorce is the only solution;

- Your son is rebellious and there is nothing that can change that behavior;

- The interviewer says there is no way the company can hire you for the job;

- You think: *"This is a curse, just like my ancestors, this is a situation that cannot be changed"*;

- You think: *"God answers only to his favorite children, and I am not one of them, that is why I don't reach His blessings and victories in my life"*;

  etc., etc., etc.

Since the mind is limited, it does not conceive how this can be reversed and ends up blocking faith and making the shell stronger. That is why the Bible teaches us in Psalms 94:11:

> "The Lord knows the thoughts of man, that they are futile".

Also, Mark 10:27 says:

> "But Jesus looked at them and said, "With man it is impossible, but not with God; for with God all things are possible."

You must break the shell of the seed of faith of the negative thoughts and opposing reasoning and arguments by believing the supernatural is going to happen, even knowing that it doesn't make sense, nor it fits in your mindset and understanding.

If you are facing any of the situations mentioned above or a different one, make the firm decision to break the shell and start believing with all your heart that the bad thoughts are not going to dominate the mind.

Neuroscience calls it neuroplasticity[1]; the capacity of the mind to choose, dominate, and change thoughts.

Let me give you an example in my own life:

> In 2011, I was diagnosed with colon cancer. The tumor was blocking 80% of the intestine passage. The oncologist said that I would have to go through

surgery and that, since the tumor was very close to the end of the intestine, there was a very high probability that they would have to permanently shut down the exit and I would have to carry a bag for the rest of my life, among other terrible side effects. Immediately my natural thoughts started to flood my mind, bringing sadness and anguish, with all the consequences I would have to face. I was only 52 years old and still had a lot to do and accomplish in my life... this was until I went to my closet to pray and was able to settle down my thoughts, took them captive, to make them obedient to Christ (according to 2 Cor. 10:4), and started to pray and believe that the Chemotherapy, the radiotherapy, and the surgery would be ok, and they would not have to perform what they predicted. I started to remember and think all the thoughts of God about healing and that brought hope and released faith to perform what God had to say about that situation.

Thank God that is exactly what happened! The surgery was very successful, God intervened, and I became cancer free and am cancer free ever since. Also, I am having absolutely normal digestion and no bag!!! Praise God!

FAITH WORS!!!

## SUGGESTED PRAYER *(say it out loud, if possible)*:

"I take total and absolute control and responsibility over my spirit, soul, and body now and cast out every thought that is blocking me to achieve my goals and what God has in store for me. I fill my mind with the thoughts God has for me, according to Jeremiah 29:11, which declares: *"For I know the plans I have for you,"* declares the LORD, *"plans to prosper you and not to harm you, plans to give you hope and a future".*

I now rebuke and eliminate every thought that is contrary to the Promises of God for my life and demolish arguments and every pretension that sets itself up against the knowledge of God, and I take captive every thought to make it obedient to Christ.

I know that God is no respecter of persons, nor does He treat people with partiality, but of all nations He accepts everyone who fears Him and does what is righteous, according to Acts 10:34,35.

I rebuke, eliminate, and totally render ineffective any and all spiritual persecution in my life and that of my descendants on account of sins and injustices committed by my ancestors. I command any and all hereditary curses to be totally eliminated from my life and my next generations in the name of Jesus.

Jesus is my Lord, and He is going to make his word be fulfilled in every area of my life, in Jesus' name, amen!

# CHAPTER 2

# UNBELIEF (Negative faith)

U nbelief is not a lack of faith, since we've seen that God has distributed faith to everyone, so unbelief is to believe the negative, that what is wished for will not happen, and the bad will happen, in opposition to what is desired, or what the bible says about it. It is agreeing with the one that came to steal, kill, and destroy, who is the devil, the father of lies. Unbelief means to direct faith to what is opposing to what should be produced, which is good and not evil, a blessing and not a curse.

To use something so powerful and wonderful given by God such as faith, and, instead of producing positive things, make it produce negative things is one of the greatest attitudes of disrespect to God and to what He has promised; it is to agree with the devil, saying that God is not good, that He does not desire what is good for us and that what the Bible teaches in Jeremiah 29:11 is not true:

*"For I know the plans I have for you, says the Lord, plans for welfare and not for evil, to give you a future and a hope".*

Unbelief blocks the operation of signs, wonders, and miracles of God, according to Matthew 13:58:

*"Now he did not do many mighty works there because of their unbelief".*

Although Jesus had all the power to perform wonderful things and produce extraordinary signs, wonders, and miracles, He was limited because of their unbelief, for they believed much more in the Jesus they saw growing up in that city than in the Jesus who was now before their eyes with all the power to perform miracles in their lives.

Jesus never said: "let it be done according to my power", but rather always said: "let it be done according to your faith"...

Since Satan is a liar and the father of lying, this means that he carries his seed like all fathers do. The male in every species is the one that carries the seed. When someone believes in the lies of the devil, he or she is choosing to let his seed germinate and produce in their minds and hearts, instead of God's seed, which is faith.

It is like shooting your own foot. It goes against what God has said and produces a terrible result, which contradicts the word of God, becoming a bad testimony and a bad report.

For example:

- You see a spot on your skin and immediately believe it is cancer, even before getting it checked;

- That the promotion or raise you are looking for is not going to happen;

- That people will abandon you;

- That money will be short, and you will have famine and lack of sustenance;

- That this is your fate, your karma: to suffer all the days of your life;

- That God is somehow mad at you and will punish you for the rest of your life;

- That this new project will not be concluded;

- That everything will go wrong in life.

Let me give you an example:

In March 2019 my wife was diagnosed with lymphoma. She had several nodules on her body. We had to act immediately. She went through chemotherapy and lost all her beautiful black hair. She became weak and could not be exposed to any bacteria or virus, so her immune system was debilitated by the treatment. Days before she started the chemotherapy, I went to the hospital to have a hernia operation, that was supposed to be releasing me in 5 days, so I would be able to take my wife to start her chemo. Unfortunately, after the operation, I had an infection and had to stay 34 days in the hospital, so my wife had to start her treatment with the help of very special friends and was not able to come and visit me, for the danger of getting any virus.

Until then, she has had a very productive and active life, counseling people, and posting a daily message of 5 minutes on Facebook and WhatsApp, that was heard by people in several countries. Now, she had to stop making and posting the audio messages, was weak, had no hair, and her husband was in the hospital, so she said that all kinds of negative thoughts came to her mind, like: "See, how God has abandoned you?" "You will not be healed", "You are worthless", "your life is over", "end up your life now, by jumping in front of an oncoming car", etc.

Instead of believing in the lies of the Devil, she decided to believe in the word of God, and praise Him, playing the piano, crying, and singing, declaring, and claiming the promises of God for her life.

After some days I was released from the hospital, she was in remission just after the 4th chemo, her beautiful hair grew back, and she is free from cancer ever since... Faith works!!!

God is good, His word is true, and he has good plans for your life. You must break the shell of faith of unbelief, if you have it, by turning the negative into positive, evil into good. God is good and you will achieve your victory!

FAITH WORKS!!!

## SUGGESTED PRAYER *(say it out loud, if possible)*:

I now take total and absolute control and responsibility over my spirit, soul, and body and rebuke from my life all the unbelief and negativity. I am what God said I am; I have what God said I have; I can do what God said I can do. God's will is sovereign in my life. He declared that by Jesus' stripes, I was healed, that I will eat the good of the land, if I am willing and obedient, which I am. Thank you, Jesus, for making my miracle a reality and by being the Lord of every area of my life! I will fulfill my days and see the works of the Lord and His will be accomplished in a supernatural and wonderful way!

I love you, Lord, and will be faithful until the end, in Jesus' name! Amen!

# CHAPTER 3

# NEGATIVE EXAMPLES
## (Bad reports)

W e can be influenced by the testimonies, stories, and reports we see and hear from other people. This can be good or bad, depending on what we see and hear. The bad report can produce a negative impact, strengthen the shell of the faith, and make us doubt that the victory will be accomplished, and the goal can be achieved. On the other hand, a good testimony can be beneficial to break the shell of the seed of faith, bringing us hope and encouragement that the goal we are seeking will be achieved, and the victory will be accomplished. We are constantly bombarded by news through images, audio, and videos through social media, TV, newspapers, and conversations, and this can be good, if we know how to filter it and only listen and hear the ones from the sources, we know to be credible and skip or shut our ears and eyes to the ones of doubtful or bad source.

Regarding social media, most of the time we can identify by the title of the video if it is good or bad, or the people or organization that is posting if it is trustworthy or not.

It is very encouraging to hear the testimony of someone that has achieved a blessing, a victory, a miracle. It edifies us, and it helps to break down the shell of the seed of faith, since it unveils the testimony of someone that overcame that obstacle.

On the other hand, a bad report is very detrimental, and can bring us discouragement and doubts, strengthening the shell of the seed of faith, and blocking it from producing.

The Psalm 101:3 is precisely what we need to put into practice more than ever:

> *"I will set nothing wicked before my eyes; I hate the work of those who fall away; It shall not cling to me".*

It is amazing how our human nature has the tendency of paying attention and considering the negative experiences more and much easier than the positive ones.

Even after witnessing victories after victories, achievements after achievements, in our own lives as well as in the lives of others, we still have the tendency to weigh down more the negative experiences, than the positive.

The Bible declares in Ephesians 5:15:

> *"Redeeming the time, because the days are evil".*

We now, more than ever, must be careful of what we see and hear, like Jesus warned, in Mark 14:38b:

*"Watch and pray so that you will not fall into temptation".*

Frustrated people can create a lot of damage to the faith. They go around spreading their frustration, influencing people to stop believing and discouraging them.

Most of the bad testimonies of the people that didn't achieve the results they were looking for are of achievements more linked to their greed and lusts they were expecting to reach that was not according to the word of God. They were thinking that they would set up whatever they wanted in their mind and God had to endorse it, doesn't matter what. They thought that whatever they wanted, they could expect and even "command" God to do. Most of the time, they didn't consider that God was protecting them by not granting the desires of their hearts and minds.

This behavior is very dangerous and places the person who thinks like this in a very slippery terrain, creating great risks for disappointments and frustrations because they don't receive everything they desire. The problem is that this kind of behavior from an individual spreads out bad news and distorts the reality of how true faith works. If we keep on listening to someone like this, we are going to be frustrated and think faith doesn't work.

You must protect your ears by filtering what you hear through the word of God. Also, one of the best ways to be protected from bad news is to avoid contact with negative and toxic people, as much as possible; those that only talk and focus on negative and destructive talking.

Look at what is written in I Corinthians 15:33:

> "Do not be misled: "Bad company corrupts good character."

I will use as an example what happened to the 12 spies that Moses sent to spy on the land they were about to conquer.

Excerpts from the book of Numbers, chapters 13 and 14:

> "They came back to Moses and Aaron and the whole Israelite community at Kadesh in the Desert of Paran. There they reported to them and to the whole assembly and showed them the fruit of the land. They gave Moses this account: "We went into the land to which you sent us, and it does flow with milk and honey! Here is its fruit. But the people who live there are powerful, and the cities are fortified and very large...
>
> Then Caleb silenced the people before Moses and said, "We should go up and take possession of the land, for we can certainly do it."
>
> But the men who had gone up with him said, "We can't attack those people; they are stronger than

we are." And they spread among the Israelites a **bad report** about the land they had explored. They said, "The land we explored devours those living in it. All the people we saw there are of great size. We saw the Nephilim there (the descendants of Anak come from the Nephilim). We seemed like grasshoppers in our own eyes, and we looked the same to them."

That night all the members of the community raised their voices and wept aloud. All the Israelites grumbled against Moses and Aaron, and the whole assembly said to them, "If only we had died in Egypt! Or in this wilderness! Why is the LORD bringing us to this land only to let us fall by the sword? Our wives and children will be taken as plunder. Wouldn't it be better for us to go back to Egypt?" And they said to each other, "We should choose a leader and go back to Egypt."

Then Moses and Aaron fell facedown in front of the whole Israelite assembly gathered there. Joshua son of Nun and Caleb son of Jephunneh, who were among those who had explored the land, tore their clothes and said to the entire Israelite assembly, "The land we passed through and explored is exceedingly good. If the LORD is pleased with us, he will lead us into that land, a land flowing with milk and honey, and will give it to us."

Out of the 12 testimonies, only 2 were positive and encouraging, stating that God would give them victory in conquering the land. The other 10 reports were terrible and discouraging, exalting the size of the men of the land. This was so hard, that everyone who heard it, started to discredit the promise God had given that they would conquer the promised land.

Pay attention to what has happened to all the ones that didn't believe, according to Jude 1:5b:

> *"...the Lord delivered his people out of Egypt. But later destroyed those who did not believe".*

This shows that God isn't playing games regarding faith and that is why, out of thousands and thousands of people, only the 2, which were Joshua and Caleb, who believed, were able to enter the promised land.

If the negative news and information is keeping you from believing, you must break that shell of the seed of faith now, confessing the word of God regarding the miracle or need you have.

FAITH WORKS!!!

## SUGGESTED PRAYER *(say it out loud, if possible)*:

I now take total and absolute control over my spirit, soul, and body and all my memories and totally and once and for all bring down and disregard every bad example, report, story, and fact that someone has shared with me, real or fictitious, or that I've read or seen somewhere. I disengage, let go, and turn ineffective all the negative feelings and emotions these reports and stories have produced in me. I uproot all of them and totally and absolutely eliminate and destroy them from my life. I am not the person that has shared the bad report with me. I am an individual whose life belongs to God and will be producing and living the miracles and wonders He has prepared for me to enjoy, in Jesus' name, amen!

# CHAPTER 4

# DOUBTS (Is it the will of God?)

The Bible declares in John 5:14:

*"This is the confidence we have in approaching God: that if we ask anything according to his will, he hears us".*

The Bible contains over 7,000 promises and displays what the will of God is with respect to the various situations in life. Ignorance to what the Bible declares concerning a certain matter creates doubts about whether that is the will of God, or not. That is why people are afraid that what they need cannot be achieved or accomplished, and therefore their faith is not put into action, that is, instead of being assured of the things they believe for, it becomes an uncertainty, so people do not accomplish the victory, because of the double mind.

God responds to prayers directed to Him, and that must be accompanied by faith.

Look what is written in James 1:6 to 8:

*"But when you ask, you must believe and not doubt, because the one who doubts is like a wave of the sea, blown and tossed by the wind. That person should not expect to receive anything from the Lord".*

If we put together the two verses written above, we conclude that, if we pray according to the will of God, believing and not doubting, He will answer.

This shows how much the knowledge of the Bible is important. When I know what God thinks and the way He acts, I will be able to break the shell of the seed of faith and accomplish tremendous results in my life.

The reason why so many prayers are not answered is because of motivation. In the book of James 4:3 and 4, we read:

*"When you ask, you do not receive, because you ask with wrong motives, that you may spend what you get on your pleasures. You adulterous people, don't you know that friendship with the world means enmity against God? Therefore, anyone who chooses to be a friend of the world becomes an enemy of God".*

The world is a system of beliefs and values. One of the most important values in the world is called "status" and "success", which is a scale used to value people according to what they have, like the car they drive, the house they live in, the clothes they wear, the jewelry they display, etc. Society respects, treats, and values individuals according to the "external signs of riches", so the greatest majority of people live according to this belief and spend their whole lives running with all their might after "things", even if this will demand a high price, and even cost their health, families, relationships, sanity, principles, conscience, moral principles, etc.

Friendship with the world means living according to the values and beliefs of the system, the "establishment". In this system, the humbleness of the heart is considered a weakness in opposition to the values God established, so people values pride, instead of humbleness. They establish their goals and targets according to their pride, expecting God to bless them and endorse their wrong motives.

Isn't that amazing that people strive to achieve "success", by acquiring things they don't need to show off to people they don't even like?

There is a difference between humbleness and poverty. Humbleness is in the heart, which means that I can have a beautiful house and great cars and still be humble, and I can live in a shack and drive an old and beaten car and still be proud.

In James 4:6 it is written:

*"But he gives us more grace. That is why Scripture says: "God opposes the proud but shows favor to the humble."*

**Humbleness** – true understanding of man's human limitations and recognition that man is totally dependent on the creator.

**Pride** – deception about human limitations and their real condition, which is just dust (Psalm 103:14), thinking that man is self-sufficient and can be independent of God.

Humbleness is a tremendous key, and it unlocks the favor of God. As a child of God, everything we have has to glorify our heavenly father, since He is the one that gave us the breath, health, opportunities, sanity, capabilities, wisdom, conditions, relationships, connections, means, etc., to achieve them, so we depend on Him to live, advance, conquer, accomplish things, and have a true and real success. God has no problem giving anyone anything, but it all depends on our motivation and if we are ready to receive what we desire.

Unfortunately, I've witnessed so many times people being so humble when they had little or few, but became so proud and self-sufficient after achieving a certain level or accomplishing wealth... this is one of the greatest deceit there is.

God is pleased when his children come before Him mentioning his Word, not demanding or in a petulant manner, but humbly believing in what he promised. He will provide what is being sought, for he fulfills his Word, according to Jeremiah 1:12:

> *"Then the Lord said to me, "I am watching over my word to perform it".*

When we pray the word of God, He is pleased. For example, He is not offended, when I pray this prayer:

"Lord, your word declares in I Peter 2:24 that by Jesus' wounds I have been healed. I believe your word is true. Thank you for taking my infirmities and my diseases on the cross, so I can be healed, in Jesus' name, Amen.

You can pray for most of the situations in your life according to the word of God the same way I've mentioned above, like:

- The will of God is to supply my needs, according to Philippians 4:19;

- The will of God is to save my family, according to Acts 16:31;

- The will of God is to give me joy, according to Philippians 4:4.

- The will of God is to forgive my sins, according to I John 1:9 and Isaiah 1:18.

- The will of God is to give me rest of all the burden I am carrying, according to Matthew 11:28-30.

- The will of God is that all things will work out for my good, according to Romans 8:28.

- The will of God is to give me eternal life, according to John 4:14.

- The will of God is to bless me with every spiritual blessing in Christ, according to Ephesians 1:3

- The will of God is to give me comfort in my trials, according to 2 Corinthians 1:3-4.

- The will of God is to give me abundant life, and to those who follow Him, according to John 10:10.

- The will of God is to enrich me in every way so that I can be generous on every occasion, according to 2 Corinthians 9:11.

If you don't know if what you need is the will of God, search His word, look for the blessings Jesus conquered for you, and break the shell of uncertainty if that is the will of God or not.

As an example, I would like to share one experience I had when a Lady came from another State to the town where we were having a prayer meeting with a small towel around her left hand. I asked what happened, and she said that she was a hairdresser and had pinched her hand with a rusted scissor, infecting it and blood and pus was coming out of the wound, and that was why she was wearing the towel around her hand. I said: do you believe the Lord Jesus

Christ has taken all your diseases in the cross, according to I Peter 2:24, and that by Jesus' wounds we have been healed, so you can be healed now? As she answered "YES", I prayed for her, and she was immediately healed. The blood and pus stopped flowing! From that moment on, nothing came out of the wound and later the wound was healed and only a scar was left. Later, she told me she was scheduled to have her arm amputated. She went back to the doctors to check if there would be no tetanus, and the result was negative!

FAITH WORKS!!!

## SUGGESTED PRAYER *(say it out loud, if possible)*:

I take total and absolute control, authority and responsibility over my spirit, soul, and body and declare that the word of God is truth and the only guidance I take to my life. I submit myself to the bible as the living word of God, which is sharper than any double-edged sword, it penetrates even to dividing my soul and my spirit; it judges the thoughts and attitudes of my heart. I humble myself before you, Father, recognizing that you are the Lord and I depend totally on you.

I am what the Bible declares that I am; I have what the Bible declares that I have; I can do what the Bible declares that I can do; I have the victory over all the darkness and evil, taking possession in my life of the work accomplished by Jesus in the cross, where he declared: "It is finished"!

There is no condemnation for me, because I am in Christ Jesus, according to Romans 8:1.

No weapon forged against me will prevail, and I will refute every tongue that accuses me. This is the heritage of the servants of the LORD, and this is my vindication from the LORD", according to Isaiah 54:17.

Jesus was pierced for my transgressions, he was crushed for my iniquities; the punishment that brought me peace was on him, and by his wounds I am healed, according to I Peter 2:24.

I Cast all my anxiety on Jesus because he cares for me, according to I Peter 5:7.

The peace of God, which transcends all understanding, will guard my heart and my mind in Christ Jesus, according to Philippians 4:7.

I receive Jesus Christ in my heart and become a child of God, by this new birth, according to John 3:3.

I commit my life to Jesus and make Him the Lord and governor of all aspects of my life, according to I Peter 3:15

I am a child of God and no longer a slave, so God sent the Spirit of His son into my heart and God has made me His heir, according to Galatians 4:6.7.

I forgive every one who has wronged me and am forgiven the same way by God, according to Matthew 6:12.

You, Lord, will keep in perfect peace those whose minds are steadfast, because they trust in you, so I am kept in perfect peace because my mind is steadfast, and I trust in you, Lord.

I believe in you and that you are faithful to fulfill your promises in my life, Lord, in Jesus' name, amen!

# CHAPTER 5

# FEELINGS AND EMOTIONS
## (Roller coaster)

We all have a soul, also called psyche, which encompasses our emotions, will, and thoughts. The soul has a high tendency of worry and to be anxious.

About all kinds of matters, mostly due to the circumstances, either in our personal lives or in our environment. Our thoughts and emotions become inundated with concerns and expectations that overwhelm us and, in so many cases make us awake all night, and take control of our emotions, mostly with the release of adrenaline, making the heart palpitate rapidly. It is impossible to mix worry and anxiety with faith: they are like water and oil, and can't be mixed. Real faith casts out all worries and anxieties and brings rest and peace.

Doesn't matter how much we get anxious or worried about something, our anxiety and worrying can't resolve the issue. When I am talking to people, I propose this exercise:

"Think about the problem that you are worried and/or anxious about. Now, try to apply to it all the anxiety or worry to the max capacity... after some minutes, I ask: Did it resolve the issue? Did the problem go away, or was even moved 1 inch towards the solution?" Every single person that does this exercise ends up saying: no, it didn't resolve anything, nor changed even a little bit.

Philippians 4:6 and 7 say:

> *"Do not be anxious about anything, but in every situation, by prayer and petition, with thanksgiving, present your requests to God. And the peace of God, which transcends all understanding, will guard your hearts and your minds in Christ Jesus".*

The person that lives in the soul realm lives in a kind of roller Coaster. Depending on the situation and the circumstances is all the way up; assured, enthusiastic, excited, and believing, when things are positive, and 5 minutes later, after receiving bad news, mainly from social media, it dives all the way down in despair, frustration, and unbelief; then up again, and down again, and so on and so forth.

The shell of the seed of faith regarding our feelings and emotions may be the hardest to break.

Just like some fruits in nature that have very hard shells, like the Brazilian nuts, which are encapsulated in a larger shell, they are like wood, very hard to break.

In Mark 9:23b, Jesus declared:

*"Everything is possible for the one who believes".*

It does not say that all things are possible to those who feel, but rather to those who believe.

How many times I've encountered people saying: "I am not feeling I will be healed", or: "I am not feeling the Lord is going to provide for my needs this month", or even: "I don't feel God really loves me"; "I don't feel I love my spouse anymore". This is the biggest deceit... believing in one's own feelings and emotions, instead of believing in what God promises and declares in His word. What is even more interesting is the volatility that the emotions produce: believing, assured, and trusting one minute and, after a negative phone call or text from someone, goes all the way to the other side doubting, frustrated, and not believing the next minute.

In Jeremiah 17:9, the Bible declares something strong:

*"The heart is deceitful above all things, and desperately corrupt; who can know it"?*

It is one of the greatest challenges we face: believing in what God has promised, even if our feelings and emotions are trying to make us doubt. Faith must overcome negative emotions and feelings for us to attain peace and the assurance that what God has promised He will fulfill.

Jesus said in Mark 11:23:

*"For assuredly, I say to you, whoever says to this mountain, 'Be removed and be cast into the sea,' and does not doubt in his heart, but believes that those things he says will be done, he will have whatever he says."*

In this verse, Jesus is emphasizing that the heart cannot be doubting, and the mouth must be saying what the heart is believing, which means that it cannot be a contradiction between them, that consistency and oneness must be clear, where the mouth is declaring what the heart is believing and the blessing will be accomplished!

Example: When I was in the hospital fighting an infection that happened because of a hernia operation, other complications started to happen, I had been at the hospital for 25 days already, so, since things started to go from bad to worse, I started to lose hope and started feeling that my life was over, that God's plans had been over in my life. This feeling started to increase and almost took over my whole heart, bringing despair and anguish. Then, I started to remember all the promises of God for my life and all the things I still knew it was for me to achieve, so, I knew it was the shell of the faith through emotions trying to take over and lead me to believe a lie. As soon as I realized it was the feelings and emotions trying to take over, I decided to break the shell and started declaring the word of God for my life, believing I would fulfill my days and accomplish all that I was created to be and do, and only die at the appointed time God has determined for my life and keep on believing until the end. At that time, I was developing an allergy to the blood thinner, among other issues, and from that point on, I started to recover, getting better, and better, and got out of the hospital in 9 days. Faith works!!!

If you are developing feelings and emotions that are contrary to what God has declared in His word, I know it is not easy, but it all starts with your understanding that your feelings can be deceiving and tricky. It all starts with a decision you have to make: either keep the feeling or rather believe the word of God.

Every feeling is followed by a thought and not the other way around. This means that we don't start feeling something out of nowhere, or out of nothing. The feeling was triggered or established by something we've remembered, something that came out of our sub-conscience, or something we were thinking at that time.

To feed the faith and make it stronger, all you must do is back your faith up with the word of God regarding your situation.

If you are feeling that what you need you are not going to receive or the miracle you need isn't going to happen, you must break this shell of the seed of faith and substitute the negative feeling for faith, even against the negative feeling or emotion you are having about it.

When you feel that anguish, sadness, bad feelings, bitterness, revolt, a desire for revenge, anger, etc. is trying to sneak into your life, even when you may have all the reason to justify those feelings, you can let them take over your whole heart or decide to break all that loose and start declaring:

"The joy of the Lord is my strength"; *(Nehemiah 8:10)*

"The Lord is not going to let any hair in my head to perish, according to Luke 21:18

"I shall not die, but I will live and see the works of the Lord and His wonders in my life"; *(Psalm 118:17)*

"Jesus already paid the price for my sins, and I don't have to carry this guilt feeling, so I forgive myself, repent and confess the sin to the Lord and believe in the wonderful forgiveness of God for all of my sins"; *(I John1:9)*

"I come to Jesus, who promised that I will find rest for my weary soul, so, I take off the heavy burden of sins and condemnation, and I take the burden of Jesus, which is light and His yoke, which is easy"; *(Matthew 11:28-30)*

"I break now all the emotions and feelings that are not aligned with the word of God and His plans for my life, and let the DNA of faith to breakthrough, which is going to bring the circumstances and situations, which are temporary and subject to change, to be transformed, and aligned to the Word of God, which is permanent and true".

FAITH WORKS!!!

If you declared in a loud voice the verses above and took possession of them in your life, they have become your prayer.

# CHAPTER 6

# SIZE OF THE PROBLEM (Mountain)

I n Matthew 17:20, we've read above, Jesus is mentioning a mountain, not a little hill, or a little mount.

> *"So, if you have faith as a mustard seed, you will say to this mountain, 'Move from here to there,' and it will move; and nothing will be impossible for you."*

When we are in front of a physical mountain, we can easily see its size and realize how minuscule we are compared to it, and our incapacity to move it. It is almost like the mountain is demanding respect from us, like stating that it won't move and there is no one to change that reality, contrary to what Jesus has declared.

When we bring this reality to our situation, sometimes we see that the challenge or the problem we are facing is so immense, that it is like a mountain: no human effort can move even 1 inch of the problem away; it is almost an impossibility. Many times, we tend to believe more readily in smaller situations than in big challenges. What Jesus is mentioning is that we will face situations in our lives that are like mountains, irremovable to our human eyes, but perfectly capable of being removed by the Lord, for what He declares in Isaiah 43:13 is this:

*"Indeed before the day was, I am He; And there is no one who can deliver out of My hand; when I act, who can reverse it"?*

If we look up to the Lord, who is the creator of all that exists, including the mountains, we conclude that He is much, much bigger than the physical and non-physical mountains, so He is absolutely capable of removing any mountain in our lives, which means that it doesn't matter how complex the situation may be, He is able to solve it. The only requirement He expects from us for his powerful hands to move is faith.

Examples of the size of the problem:

- Believe in the cure of a headache vs. belief for the cure of cancer;
- Believe in the miracle for $1,000.00 vs. believe in the miracle for $100,000.00 or more;

- Believe in the solution of little marital discords, vs. believe in the restoration of a marriage, even after the divorce papers have been signed and the couple is already apart from each other.

Since the mountain is much bigger than us, we have the natural tendency to think it is too big to be removed. Of course, the miracle we need is very big or the problem we are facing is very complicated to resolve, but our focus must be placed on the power of God, which is much stronger and bigger than any mountain or situation we face, or miracle we need.

The size of the problem or challenge can be so overwhelming, it can end up in a depression. According to the World Health Organization, depression is the leading cause of mental disorders, and its definition is "an illness characterized by persistent sadness and a loss of interest in activities that you normally enjoy, accompanied by an inability to carry out daily activities, for at least two weeks. The Oxford Language defines depression as Feelings of severe despondency and dejection. This means that the person feels incapable of solving the problem(s) and finding a solution to the situation, feeling despair, which can escalate to depression. If this is your situation, it must be properly diagnosed, so seek out help from a professional in the area.

Example: I've asked permission from a dear friend that we've known since 1991 to share her testimony because it is very strong and illustrates how a huge mountain can be removed from our lives. Her name is Kathy. When she was 33 years old, she was diagnosed with lupus, which was an incurable disease. The first thing she did was to ask the church to start praying for her. She was submitted to the proper treatment, but her kidneys began to fail after some time and some other complications led the doctors to tell her that there was nothing else they could do about the case and that she would have to face the reality of death. Kathy was born and raised in Brazil, where most of her family lives, so she was able to contact a doctor in that country and he offered to try to help her situation. When she was about to leave the USA, another common friend of ours visited her to say goodbye, without any hope that she would be able to survive, so it was mostly a farewell. After arriving in Brazil, the doctor concluded that nothing else could be done for her and had her admitted to the hospital, trying to have them provide the most comfort for the rest of her time. The disease took its course, and her mind was affected up to a point when she was so agitated, that she had to be tied to her bed frame. Even in this challenging situation, (a huge mountain) the churches both in Brazil and the USA were praying, interceding for her life. The doctors told the family it was time for them to start the preparations for her funeral. After some days, she went into a coma and, after 15 days of being in that condition, she had a dream where she was lying down at her hospital bed and started to look up, where a very radiant light started to shine, and she heard the voice of her name that was being written in a little stone. As soon as the dream finished, she woke up from the coma and started to talk. Her son was preparing to go to Brazil for her funeral, but when he arrived there, she was being released from the hospital. It took a while for her mind to fully recover and after that, she went to the doctors, and they were astonished to see that there was no lupus nor any trace of it in her body at all! Now she lives a normal life, enjoying her precious family and giving her testimony to various people. Faith works!

If you are facing a mountain in front of you, break the shell of the seed of faith and start believing in God and His might and power and start declaring that the mountain will be removed, the miracle you need will happen, and the situation you are facing will be resolved.

FAITH WORKS!!!

## SUGGESTED PRAYER *(say it out loud, if possible)*:

I take total and absolute control and responsibility over my spirit, soul, and body and acknowledge that the size of the mountain in front of me is huge and that I can't, by my own strength and wisdom remove it, so I now acknowledge that God is much bigger, stronger, and mightier than the mountain and He is capable to remove it. Independently on what form the mountain may present itself, either as an illness, a relationship discord, a financial difficulty, an addiction, or any other challenge in front of me, I now believe and declare that it will be removed and cast into the sea, never to come back and be formed again.

I believe with my heart and declare with my mouth that there is nothing impossible for my God to do and change. God is capable, able, willing, and absolutely strong and wise enough to transform defeat into victory, trouble into solution, the bad into good, and the impossible into possible. His majestic and sovereign authority takes control of the situation that I am facing and changes it from a curse to a blessing, in Jesus' name, amen!

# CHAPTER 7

# FOCUS ON THE PROBLEM
## (Staring at the wrong place)

In Romans 4:19 through 21 we read the following about Abraham:

> *"And not being weak in faith, he did not consider his own body, already dead (since he was about a hundred years old), and the deadness of Sarah's womb. He did not waver at the promise of God through unbelief, but he was strengthened in faith, giving glory to God, and being fully convinced that what He had promised He was also able to perform".*

These verses are showing where Abraham, the father of faith, was putting his attention. It was not in an empty crib, crying and asking why the Lord never fulfilled his promises to give them a son... or He was late fulfilling them... but rather he was directing his attention to the one who promised, which is God.

When we focus our attention on the problem, we are showing that the problem is more important than God, who has promised us victory.

Abraham could have pitied himself and murmured against God and what He had promised for 25 years, but he opted to simply believe. I believe that at night he would go out and gaze at the stars in the sky, rejoicing and praising God for the families on earth that would be blessed through him, according to what God has promised.

If we focus on the problem, it seems as if that is all we can see before us, it feeds our questioning and unbelief, instead of our faith.

Have you ever encountered the type of individual that seems to have nothing else to talk about except his/her problem? You meet this type of individual on Sunday morning and, as soon as they greet you, they begin to talk about the problem that afflicts them. Afterward or even another day, you run into them again and once again they mention the problem. This shows a behavioral habit that demonstrates the individual is giving importance to the problem and doubting God, who had already promised victory. This only weakens faith.

Several times, I have observed individuals who, shortly after laying down their problems at the feet of Jesus, believing that God will resolve them, do see their problems resolved. It is like what I've heard sometimes about a woman who wants to conceive and that is all she talks about every time she meets someone, but then decides to no longer focus on her problem but to put her trust in God, stops talking about it and soon after she conceives!

The spiritual world is more real than the physical world, and it influences it in a very real way.

The spiritual world sees what our natural eyes can't. Nothing can be hidden from it since all is clear and open to it.

We can't deceive God, saying we believe, but act differently. For example, the reason for what happened to Job was fear, according to his own words. He sacrificed animals to the Lord in his children's name, even though they did not even know or agreed with it. He was afraid the wrath of God could be brought to them, so he thought that by sacrificing in their name, God would be merciful to them. He thought only he knew about this fear, but all is clear to the spiritual realm, so his fear created a spiritual argument and Satan knew it, pointing it out to God that, if He would take away his family, and other things he had that brought him security, Job would curse Him.

We can say or act like we really believe in the promises of God or try just to pretend we believe, thinking God is not paying attention or can be deceived. This is a very dangerous situation, since it is hypocrisy, which is worse than being sincere with God, saying we need help on our unbelief, like the father of that boy that was demon-possessed, in Mark 9:24:

*"Immediately the boy's father exclaimed: "I do believe, help me overcome my unbelief!"*

Where are you putting your focus? Is it in the problem or in the Lord that has promised victory, like Abraham?

For example, I remember years after I got my license as a business broker, I was invited to be the vice president of an American Company. We were bringing the endowment fund of Harvard University and Prudential Insurance (timber division-Prutimber) to invest in Brazil. In the 14 months it took to do all the negotiations and go through the whole process, the deal fell apart 4 times! Each time it encountered a dead end, it was looking like it would be impossible for it to be resurrected. I was impacted by the situation but refused to believe in what looked like, but rather in the God that has brought me and my family back down to Brazil for a reason, and that this deal would go through and I would be rewarded  for all the stress, work, and countless hours of meeting after meeting we had to have; translating, negotiating, learning, gathering all the information, traveling, discussing all the details, overcoming all the cultural and legal differences between the two countries, trying to make the "meeting of the minds", etc., etc. God is faithful and all the effort and faith were rewarded when the deal finally closed and went through! Keeping the focus on the one that made the promise pays off! Faith works!

If this is your situation, you must break this shell of the seed of faith by re-directing your attention away from the problem to the One that had promised the miracle to happen.

FAITH WORKS!!!

## SUGGESTED PRAYER *(say it out loud, if possible)*:

I take total and absolute authority and responsibility over my spirit, soul, and body now, and take my attention and eyes from the problem and the negative situation and turn all my attention, mind, and focus to the God that has made His promises and gave me power and authority to trample on snakes and scorpions and to overcome all the power of the enemy; nothing will harm me. Jesus has overcome the enemy of my soul because He is stronger than him, and He has overpowered Satan and taken away the armor in which he trusted and divided up his plunder with me. I now believe and declare the promises that God has made to be the only reality. My life belongs to my Lord Jesus, and I will see all His promises being fulfilled in my life, in Jesus' name, amen!

# CHAPTER 8

# FEAR (Overtaken by this feeling)

F ear is a feeling that can help and protect us from some dangers, fear keeps people from diving into a river that they don't know its depth or what is at its bottom, which could hurt or even kill them; protects the professional that works fixing power lines by using the proper equipment to do his work; it prevents the children from lying to the parents, afraid they will be disciplined, etc.

On the other hand, there is the negative side of fear, which is the fear of moving forward, achieving, conquering goals and targets in life. I've seen and heard the results of interviews with older people many times when they answered what they regret the most in their lives, and the number one answer is: I should risk more, I should try to pursue new projects and try to achieve some dreams more. It was fear of the unknown that kept them from moving forward. Fear can paralyze, it can take over the person and even become a syndrome, or phobia, like night terror syndrome.

There is a misconception that people have about the difference between "fear" and "concern". I can have faith for something, even when I am concerned and aware of its hurdles and possible mishaps. Considering all the possibilities, challenges, and obstacles that I will have to overcome is healthy, positive, and even needed. For example, if I believe that I should be opening a new business, I must do it by faith but also must consider all the challenges and obstacles I will have to face.

Look at what Jesus said, in Mark 5:36:

*"But ignoring what they said, Jesus said to the ruler of the Synagogue, "Do not fear, only believe".*

Fear is a strong aversion to the pain a disappointment, rejection, or frustration may create. Just thinking about what an individual may feel because of a disappointment, in case what is desired does not happen, that individual prefers to give up believing, preferring to lose the blessing rather than "risking" believing and being disappointed.

An interesting example of this is found in Psalms 107:23 through 30:

*"Those who go down to the sea in ships, who do business on great waters, they see the works of the Lord, and His wonders in the deep. For He commands and raises the stormy wind, which lifts up the waves of the sea. They mount up to the heavens, they go down again to the depths; Their soul melts because of trouble. They reel to and fro, and stagger like a drunken man, and are at their wits' end. Then they cry out to the Lord in their trouble, And He brings them out of their distresses. He calms the storm, so that its waves are still. Then they are glad because they are quiet; so, He guides them to their desired port"*

This passage illustrates very well how faith leads us to "see the works of the Lord and His wonders in the deep". First, we must overcome fear and decide to navigate, untying our boat from the dock, which represents our comfort zone, our safe haven. In the beginning, all seems normal, and we are enthusiastic about reaching our goal, which is crossing to the other side. Then God sends the winds and adversities our way, like waves that mount up to heaven, taking us to the heights, where we are encouraged and we can see everything from above, thinking that we are at the top and exalted by God, when suddenly the wave takes a downturn, and we find ourselves at the very bottom, discouraged and regretting having left our comfort zone and we start to miss it. All of this serves to break the structure of independence, pride, and self-exaltation of our flesh. That is when, after clearly seeing our fragility, our anguish for not being able to resolve the problem, we cry out to God asking Him to help us. It is when we are humbled and recognize our total and absolute dependency on Him, and it is then that He makes the waves calm down, the wind to stop, and then takes us to the safe port that we desire to reach.

I Corinthians 1:29 shows that God does not accept boasting of the flesh, because it is deceitful:

*"That no flesh should glory in His presence".*

Necessity is the greatest motivator there is. To desire something is very different than to need something. Necessity creates in us a strong tenacity and motivation to obtain what we need, facing challenges, barriers, and oppositions that present themselves before us.

Even if during the storm the thought of returning to our comfort zone comes to our mind, we do not accept it and we continue pressing on forward.

Example: When I started working in the US as a horse dentist, it was a huge challenge, due to my broken English, and fear people would not accept a guy coming from the third world offering some techniques and equipment that were unknown to the Americans, etc. While doing routine dental treatment on a horse, in 1994, a gentleman asked if I could fix the bite of a mare that had severe overbite. That was something totally new to me and there was no literature in the world about it or any way to learn it from someone. At that time, there were no personal computers, the internet, Google, Bing, A.I., Chat GPT, etc. That was a challenge that I had to overcome and develop a way to fix the problem by myself. So, I decided to overcome the fear, and after praying a lot, thinking a lot, and planning a lot on how to do it, even concerned about the possible unknown results, I decided to accept the challenge and started fixing horse's bite with braces, both under and overbite (upper and lower jaw). Since then, I've stopped counting when I've reached the 160th animal fixed.

FAITH WORKS!

Fear must be broken. Only faith can lead us to conquests, victories, and accomplishments.

The shell of the seed of faith must be broken regarding fear. It is a bold and courageous decision. It is when you take a stand and say: — *"Enough is enough, I am living in fear for so long, missing the best God has for me! From now on I will believe what God states in His word and declare it for my life"!*

FAITH WORKS!!!

## SUGGESTED PRAYER *(say it out loud, if possible)*:

I take total and absolute control and authority over my spirit, soul, and body and hereby declare that fear and any kind of phobia are out of my life, and I command it to leave my mind and my emotions never to come back. I substitute all the fear with faith, which overcomes all the fear. I shield my life with the full armor of God, including the helmet of salvation and the shield of faith, which extinguishes all the flaming arrows of the evil one. I extinguish the darts of threats that the devil is trying to throw at me and my mind, using the shield of faith.

I am aware of the challenges and obstacles that I will have to overcome and believe that, by faith, I will accomplish the supernatural and unbelievable at human eyes and understanding. I declare that fear is no longer in control of my life and believe that all God has in store for me I will achieve and accomplish, in Jesus' name, amen!

# CHAPTER 9

# PASSIVITY (Apathy)

The courage to face the situation and do something about it displays the behavior of a real soldier. Passive people act like cowards, they see the problem, but don't do a thing about it. Conformity to circumstances is one of the most frequent reasons why individuals do not move forward and end up not seeing the fulfillment of the promises of God in their lives and the achievement of their goals. These are the people who say, "That's the way it is, nothing changes, I was born this way, my father was this way, my grandfather was this way, and I am destined to be this way, too".

Bartimaeus had an attitude that displays how the non-conformity with the situation and even the social pressure granted him the victory and the achievement he was looking for. It is registered in Mark 10:47 to 52:

*"And when he heard that it was Jesus of Nazareth, he began to cry out and say: "Jesus, Son of David, have mercy on me!" Then many warned him to be quiet; **but he cried out all the more**, "Son of David, have mercy on me! Jesus stopped and said, "Call him." So they called to the blind man, "Cheer up! On your feet! He's calling you." Throwing his cloak aside, he jumped to his feet and came to Jesus. "What do you want me to do for you?" Jesus asked him. The blind man said, "Rabbi, I want to see." "Go," said Jesus, "your faith has healed you." Immediately he received his sight and followed Jesus along the road."*

He was not deterred by those who rebuked him that told him to be silent, but rather he cried out "all the more" until he received the miracle. Obviously, those who told him to be quiet were not blind, because if they were, they would cry out as much or more than he did.

Passive individuals seek the greater number of excuses and justifications possible to not advance and to explain to their own conscience the reason why they do not move forward and do not receive the promises of God. Mediocrity is its greatest characteristic. This type of individual "feeds" his own conscience with the defeat of others, enjoying hearing stories about weaknesses and failures, seeking to appease his own conscience in the event someone asks for the reason for such great laziness, passiveness, and ostracism on their lives.

Some of these people believe in "karma", that is, that their fate is that way and nothing will help change that picture. Others believe in the absurdity of paying the debt of sins and mistakes committed in some past life and that this must be paid, when the bible doesn't endorse re-incarnation, according to Hebrews 9:27:

*"Just as people are destined to die once, and after that to face judgment".*

For example, I will quote what happened with the officer of the King, when Samaria was besieged:

*"Ben-Hadad king of Aram mobilized his entire army and marched up and laid siege to Samaria. There was a great famine in the city; the siege lasted so long that a donkey's head sold for eighty shekels of silver, and a quarter of a cab of seed pods for five shekels...*

*The king said, "This disaster is from the LORD. Why should I wait for the LORD any longer?" Elisha replied, "Hear the word of the LORD. This is what the LORD says: About this time tomorrow, a seah of the finest flour will sell for a shekel and two seahs of barley for a shekel at the gate of Samaria." The officer on whose arm the king was leaning said to the man of God, **"Look, even if the LORD should open the floodgates of the heavens, could this happen?"** "You will see* *it with your own eyes," answered Elisha, "but you will not eat any of it!"*

*... later, the people went out and plundered the camp of the Arameans. So a seah of the finest flour sold for a shekel, and two seahs of barley sold for a shekel, as the LORD had said. Now the king had put the officer on whose arm he leaned in charge of the gate, and the people trampled him in the gateway, and he died, just as the man of God had foretold when the king came down to his house..."*

You can see that the officer was so used to the situation that was taking so long, that he became passive about it, in such a way that when the prophet brought the revelation, he opposed it, fiercely. The whole city was blessed and saved, but he didn't participate in the victory and died.

If passivity is your problem, you need to understand that faith is active, not something that makes things and miracles just happen by themselves, but it requires an action on our part, so break this shell of the seed of faith and do what the bible tells us in Ephesians 5:14:

*"This is why it is said: "Wake up, sleeper, rise from the dead, and Christ will shine on you."*

FAITH WORKS!!!

**SUGGESTED PRAYER** *(say it out loud, if possible)*:

I take total and absolute authority over my spirit, soul, and body and take the position of the soldier that I was called to be, belonging to the army of God. I stand up and salute my Lord of hosts, Jesus Christ. I rebuke all the plots and temptations that try to paralyze me, and now I neutralize all the passiveness, feeling of undeserving, laziness, feeling down, inferiority, desire to give up, desire to give in, guilt, shame, and sleepiness of my life, and I take the position of authority, courage, and boldness against all the plots of the enemy, and take a stand against them, scolding them out of my life, never to come back again, in Jesus' name, amen.

# CHAPTER 10

# LACK OF RESILIENCE
# (Fainting, weakening)

F aith is like a muscle and needs to be exercised to develop. If we do not put faith into practice, it becomes inactive. Many times, the miracle does not happen immediately; it requires persistence and perseverance. Abraham persisted in faith for 25 years until he received the fulfillment of the promise.

Persistence and perseverance are very important actions that make our faith grow and to be productive. Jesus told a parable that demonstrates this in Luke 11:5 through 9:

> *"And He said to them, "Which of you shall have a friend, and go to him at midnight and say to him, 'Friend, lend me three loaves; for a friend of mine has come to me on his journey, and I have nothing*

*to set before him'; and he will answer from within and say, 'Do not trouble me; the door is now shut, and my children are with me in bed; I cannot rise and give to you'? I say to you, though he will not rise and give to him because he is his friend, yet because of his persistence he will rise and give him as many as he needs. "So I say to you, ask, and it will be given to you; seek, and you will find; knock, and it will be opened to you. For everyone who asks receives, and he who seeks finds, and to him who knocks it will be opened".*

It was because of the persistence of the person that was asking, that his friend stood up and helped him.

At the end of this passage, Jesus mentions 3 types of attitudes: **ask**, **seek**, and **knock**. These are attitudes that define how determined and persistent we are. If we only ask, we limit our faith. The following step is another attitude: seek. If we still ask and do not receive, we seek. If we seek and do not find, we knock, so that the blessing is received. These 3 attitudes will develop the "muscle" of our faith.

It is interesting to see how much people persist and persevere, depending on the situation and the motivation. The majority take up hard orders and commands from their bosses and persist and persevere, sometimes in a hostile environment, because they are motivated by the money, they depend on to survive and pay bills or maybe the career they are trying to build up. Others persevere in calling someone they fell in love with, sending messages, buying gifts, do everything to conquer that person's heart, motivated by the passion they are feeling.

The problem is that some people read this book about faith or hear someone talking about this subject today and think their miracle or answer to their prayers will come the next morning. If it doesn't happen, they just give up believing and do not persist and persevere, believing what they need will never come.

We are the generation of fast food, smartphones, fast cars, and microwaves and don't have the patience older generations had. They had to work hard to prepare and cook their food, send letters or telegrams which took a long time to be answered, and walk long distances to get somewhere. We want things to happen immediately, or we give up believing.

Let me give you an example:

When my wife was diagnosed with lymphoma, we immediately started asking for the Lord to heal her supernaturally. The situation required a prompt response to the problem, since we didn't get the answer for supernatural healing by asking, we started seeking it by going to physicians to have the diagnosis confirmed. After that, we went to knocking, looking for proper treatment. We exercised the faith the whole time, via asking, seeking, and knocking until we received the miracle we were looking for.

Resilience is the capacity to withstand or to recover quickly from difficulties, it is developing toughness. Perseverance and patience are keys to accomplishing the blessings God has for your life.

See what David declares in Psalm 40:1:

*"I waited patiently for the LORD; he turned to me and heard my cry".*

The prophet Isaiah, in the 40th chapter, verses 29 to 31 of his book, shows the secret to reaching the highest places:

*"He gives strength to the weary and increases the power of the weak. Even youths grow tired and weary, and young men stumble and fall;* **but those who hope in the LORD will renew their strength.** *They will soar on wings like eagles; they will run and not grow weary; they will walk and not be faint".*

Jesus has mentioned that perseverance is necessary for the fruit to be produced, in Luke 8:15:

*"But the seed on good soil stands for those with a noble and good heart, who hear the word, retain it, and* **by persevering** *produce a crop".*

The Bible displays the difference between our time of 24 hours, calling it Chronos, and God's time, which is called Kairos, which is set forth by God. The difference between them is that we live in the Chronos and, at the appointed time (Kairos), the projects and plans I have that came from God will be fulfilled. Some happen in a very short time, but others take a little longer.

Let me give you an example:

When I was 16 years of age, a friend invited me to go to a prayer meeting. When we were praying, a prophetess came and started praying for me and gave me a word that I would be a pastor. That filled my heart with joy and faith. At such young age, I didn't have what it takes to become a pastor but thought it would happen the next week or month. The Lord prepared me for eight years until I was finally able to be ordained at the age of 24. All those years the Lord was developing in me the patience, resilience, and tenacity I had to have for me to become a shepherd of a flock, responsible to teach, counseling, disciple, correcting, edifying, rebuking, praying with, preach to, listen to, be meek and, at the same time, have authority to properly develop the ministry. It required a lot of perseverance and persistence, but the fruits came through.

Another example of resilience, through perseverance and persistence: In 1985, I was asked to minister in the home of Mrs. Lina, who gave her life to Jesus when visiting her son, who was a member of the church I was the pastor of. She lived in Campo Grande, the State Capital of Mato Grosso do Sul, 625 miles from my home, and highways were narrow, and very dangerous at that time. After praying and preparing to go, I was very happy to minister there to her friends, and family, 9 in total in her very humble house. This was on May 5th of that year. The move of God was so wonderful, that they asked me to come back. After my leadership's approval, I started a home group meeting that would meet every month, so I've had the privilege to commit to minister there, even while pastoring my home church. While I was serving there, I was humbled to baptize people, visit them, minister to their lives, help with their needs, etc...

Sometimes, for one reason or another, there were just very few people, like 6 or 7, which made me wonder if it was worth it for me to travel 625 miles one way to have such few people in the meeting. When I've asked the Lord, His response was that, if I did it for 10 years and only 1 person was saved, it was worthed.

After doing it monthly for 2 years, thank God, the group grew in number, reaching an attendance of around 40 people, and my wife and I decided to move to that beautiful city with our 3 small children. I was able to make a living by working in my animal dentistry practice, fixing horses' and cattle's teeth. After staying in that city for 2,5 years, establishing, and organizing the church, the attendance grew up in numbers, reaching an attendance of around 75/80 people. At that time, we understood it was time to move to the US and left another pastor to replace me.

This new pastor was very persistent and persevered so much in prayers and dedication to pastoring the church, that it grew over all these years, reaching in 2023 the number of over 6,000 local members and 10 congregations. Several leaders have been formed and grown in that ministry, which is impacting the city and several parts of the nation. Thank God! Resilience strengthens faith and breaks the shell that sometimes tries to make us stop and give up. Faith works!

You must break the shell of the seed of faith of immediate expectations and keep on believing with patience! Develop resilience and you will see and accomplish mighty and great things in your life!

It is important to mention that God's timing is not like ours. We must maintain an attitude of faith, even when our answer seems to be delayed. God's timing is perfect, and He always answers prayers. I have some goals in my life that I am still praying to achieve but, even after breaking all the shells, for some reason I didn't achieve them, but keep on believing I will achieve them.

Let's see what the apostle Paul said in Galatians 6:9:

> *"Let us not become weary in doing good, for at the proper time we will reap a harvest if we do not give up".*

This verse applies also to our faith...we must keep on believing, until the proper time, which, in this verse is Kairos, which is God's time, and we will reap!

FAITH WORKS!!!

## SUGGESTED PRAYER *(say it out loud, if possible)*:

I take total and absolute responsibility and authority over my spirit, soul, and body and rebuke from my life all the anxiety to have my plans and goals achieved. Now, I break the frustration, the desire to give up, and the despair from my heart, and substitute them with enthusiasm, hope, and trust that the God of all grace, who called me to his eternal glory in Christ, after I have suffered a little while, will himself restore me and make me strong, firm, and steadfast. I cast out all the lack of vision and everything that is trying to make me stop believing. Forgetting what is behind and straining toward what is ahead, I press on toward the goal to win the prize for which God has called me heavenward in Christ Jesus.

I will reach my goal and fulfill the purpose I was born to fulfill, in Jesus' name, Amen!

# CHAPTER 11

# BAD CONSCIENCE (Self-righteousness vs. God's grace)

A bad conscience is always judgmental and can't accept the grace and forgiveness God is offering to whoever repents and confess their sins.

I John 3:20 through 22 declares:

> *"know that, if our heart condemns us, greater is God than our heart, and He knows all things. Beloved, if our heart does not condemn us, we trust in God, and anything we ask of Him, we will receive, because we keep His commandments and we do what is pleasing in His sight."*

The person that keeps a condemning attitude, won't believe that will receive anything from the Lord, because the conscience will keep on saying that he/she doesn't deserve God's favor or blessings, because of sin and guilt.

If we don't believe in the forgiveness of the Lord, we are denying the power of the blood of Jesus, not believing in what the bible declares in I John 1:9:

*"If we confess our sins, He is faithful and just to forgive us our sins and to cleanse us from all unrighteousness."*

God's justice isn't like ours. We think that if we fail once or twice, or even after having promised we would never sin again and fail, we are not worthy or don't deserve God's forgiveness. Underestimating God's grace is throwing away the price Jesus paid on the cross for our sins. His grace isn't a permit to sin, but it extends to us the undeserved favor of forgiveness and freedom from guilt and condemnation.

Even if we have terrible sins, like Saul, who consented to the murder of Christians, the blood of Jesus is sufficient to cleanse us from all shame and guilt.

Even in the Old Testament, the Lord promises forgiveness, independent of how dark the sins were, according to Isaiah 1:16 to 18:

*"Wash and make yourselves clean. Take your evil deeds out of my sight; stop doing wrong. Learn to do right; seek justice. Defend the oppressed. Take up the cause of the fatherless; plead the case of the widow. "Come now, let us settle the matter," says the LORD. "Though your sins are like scarlet,*

*they shall be as white as snow; though they are*
*red as crimson, they shall be like wool".*

Take a second look at verses 21 and 22 of 1 John chapter 3. It shows that, if our heart doesn't condemn us, we trust in God, which means that we believe, and we will receive anything we ask of him.

As an example, I want to point out the difference between Judas and Peter.

Judas betrayed Jesus and had remorse for doing it, which is different than repenting.

This situation about Judas is registered in Matthew 27:3:

*"When Judas, who had betrayed him, saw that*
*Jesus was condemned, he was seized with **remorse***
*and returned the thirty pieces of silver to the chief*
*priests and the elders".*

The original word for remorse is "metamelomai", which indicates a regret that has no intention or actions for redemption.

The situation about Peter is registered in Matthew 26:75:

*"Then Peter remembered the word Jesus had*
*spoken: "Before the rooster crows, you will disown*
*me three times." And he went outside and wept*
*bitterly".*

The word for repentance is "metanoia", which means "change of mind and purpose", which requires true brokenness.

There is a big difference between remorse and repentance. Remorse doesn't show a way out or a solution, while repentance shows that there is a solution for the sin that has been committed.

In II Corinthians 7:10, the Bible clearly shows this difference:

> *"Godly sorrow brings repentance that leads to salvation and leaves no regret (remorse), but worldly sorrow brings death..."*

When Jesus quoted Matthew 13:42, he referred to remorse:

> *"They will throw them into the blazing furnace, where there will be weeping and gnashing of teeth".*

The weeping is not of repentance, for there is no way out of the situation for the people who have been cast into hell, no way to be forgiven and restored. There is remorse, which means that the memory of the wrongdoing keeps rewinding and rewinding and there is no way out of that situation.

Be careful not to listen to the accuser, stating that there is no solution for your sin or that God can't forgive you. This creates a spiral that keeps on spinning in the person's mind as not seeing that the full price has been already paid and that all sins will be forgiven, according to Hebrews 8:12:

*"For I will forgive their wickedness and will remember their sins no more."*

I have encountered and spoken with backsliders that for one reason, or another have left the church and the Christian faith. The majority were due to being frustrated by the leaders of the church or someone else's action that upset them so much that they just decided not to ever go back. Their situation is like the ember that is taken out of the flames or heat that is produced when all the charcoal is together and put aside... in a little while it becomes cold again...

If for any reason you have left the church and the fellowship and started doing and saying things you didn't suppose to, you should understand that God has a plan for those who left the original plan. He is the God of second chances and is willing and totally able to forgive you and restore your life and communion with Him and His flock.

If you are not forgiving yourself or not believing the forgiveness God is willing to freely grant you, break this shell of the seed of faith now and take control of your own bad conscience, believing in the promises of God, stating that He forgives the sin and cleanses from all unrighteousness.

Hebrews 10:22b states:

*"... having our hearts sprinkled to cleanse us from a guilty (or bad) conscience".*

Bad conscience must be out of your heart for you to move forward with your life. You must stop accepting the accusations and appreciate the value of the blood that was shed on that cross for you!

FAITH WORKS!!!

## SUGGESTED PRAYER *(say it out loud, if possible)*:

I take total and absolute authority and responsibility over my spirit, soul, and body and repent of my sins, faults, shortcomings, offenses, judgments, accusations, fails and any and all the actions or thoughts I've done or had, along with the actions I should've taken, but didn't, and repent and confess now to you, Lord, asking you to forgive all my sins and cleanse me entirely with the powerful blood of Jesus Christ. I believe you have a plan for me and ask you to forgive me to have left the right way and path you had planned and repent and returning to the point I've made the wrong turn.

Thank you for forgiving me and for not remembering my sins and for accepting me back to your arms of love, as my heavenly Abba, my dear father. In Jesus' name, amen!

# CHAPTER 12
# SKEPTICISM
# (Fortress in the mind)

Skepticism is a pre-conceived idea that becomes a fortress in people's mind. It doesn't matter how many arguments, explanations, or discussions someone brings or presents to the skeptic, he or she will not conceive or appease the idea of changing their mind, even when they are proved wrong. It is linked to stubbornness, a behavior that leads to isolation and social uproars. Stubbornness is different than persistence. It is forcing someone to think and behave her or his own way, even after it has been exposed and proven to be wrong by family members, spouses, colleagues, and relatives, all trying to convince the person, but still to no avail.

The Bible mentions this fortress in 2 Corinthians 10:4 and 5:

*"The weapons we fight with are not the weapons of the world. On the contrary, they have divine power to demolish strongholds. We demolish arguments and every pretension that sets itself up against the knowledge of God, and we take captive every thought to make it obedient to Christ".*

The biggest challenge we face today when sharing the Word of God is the spirit of skepticism that is in the world today. People simply doubt and challenge everything. The worst situation is even inside so many churches, where faith in the supernatural has been replaced with doubt and unbelief, making preachers must go into lengthy sermons and a lot of reasoning to prove that God is still alive and that He still performs what He has promised.

To demolish strongholds, we should use the proper tools. The word of God is this tool, according to Jeremiah 23:29:

*"Is not my word like fire," declares the LORD, "and like a hammer that breaks a rock in pieces?*

It is a ridiculous situation when someone tries to oppose or even contend with the Creator of the universe and what he has established as truth. We are like dust, a little grain of sand, compared to God. He was, is, and always will be.

We need to examine and meditate on the word of God and substitute our old thinking with it, as it is written in Romans 12:2:

*"Do not conform to the pattern of this world but be transformed by the renewing of your mind. Then you will be able to test and approve what God's will is — his good, pleasing, and perfect will".*

Only when we get rid of our skepticism, accept, and believe in the word of God, and have our minds renewed, we will be able to be set free, according to the words of Jesus, in John 8:31 and 32:

*"To the Jews who had believed him, Jesus said, "If you hold to my teaching, you are really my disciples. Then you will know the truth, and the truth will set you free."*

Real freedom sets us free through the knowledge of the truth.

Sometimes, skepticism is associated with sarcasm, which is defined as ridicule or mockery used harshly, often crudely and contemptuously, for destructive purposes.

So many times, we see in the broad media, among circles, and social media the mockery about the Bible, God, Jesus, religion, etc. Jokes are shared among people to make fun of things and people that should be respected and never be mocked or ridiculed.

This mockery comes from the devil, with the evil intention to twist the holy into common, the light into darkness, the good into bad, the supernatural and beautiful into rational and undesirable.

As an example of people who got rid of their skepticism and converted to believers, I want to mention 2:

Saul, who later became Paul, the apostle, was persecuting the church and arresting the Christians, as he had a supernatural encounter on his way to Damascus, where he was heading to arrest more Christians. A very bright light came with a voice that said: Saul, Saul, why do you persecute me? "Who are you, Lord?" Saul asked. "I am Jesus, whom you are persecuting," Jesus replied. After that powerful encounter, he changed completely and became an apostle, preaching the gospel in several places, performing miracles and wonders, and writing a great portion of the New Testament.

The second one I want to mention is Sir William Mitchell Ramsay. He was a highly respected archaeologist from Scotland. He set out to prove the historical inaccuracies of the Book of Acts. 15 years he spent researching and digging, only to end up being convinced of the incredible accuracy of the book, converted to Christianity, and called Luke (who wrote Acts) one of the greatest historians to ever lived. He has written several books on the subject, which have yet to be refuted. His work caused an outcry from atheists because they had been eagerly awaiting his results in disproving the validity of the book.

I can mention many other famous people, like Dr. Simon Greenleaf, C. S. Lewis (Clive Staples Lewis), Gerald L. Schroeder, Professor William F. Albright, Professor Nelson Glueck, Lee Strobel, Andre Kole, Josh McDowell, etc. all respected people that started as skeptical, but later broke up the skepticism and decided to believe.

Get rid of skepticism that is keeping your faith to produce a wonderful, fruitful, and blessed life that has been planned for you to enjoy!

FAITH WORKS!!!

## SUGGESTED PRAYER *(say it out loud, if possible)*:

I take total and absolute control and responsibility over my spirit, soul, and body and rebuke and cast out from my life all the skepticism and resistance that raises up against the knowledge of Christ and totally destroy the fortress that has been built in my mind blocking me to receive and accomplish all that God has planned for my life. I believe the word of God is truth and no thought, sarcasm, joke, doubt, or cynicism can or will block me from moving forward and accomplishing all that I was born to accomplish, reaching the goals, and fulfilling my purpose, in Jesus' name, amen!

# CHAPTER 13

# NEGATIVE CONFESSION (Wrong spoken words)

Our words have the power of life and death, according to Proverbs 18:21:

*"The tongue has the power of life and death, and those who love it will eat its fruit"*

In my life, I have counseled and ministered personally to hundreds of people. It is amazing how the words spoken by someone have the power to bless or curse.

Those people who are always saying: "My life is worthless" or "I am a disgrace", or even: "I want to die" or "I won't accomplish anything in my life" are attracting to their lives the negative that they are confessing with their lips.

In Matthew 12:34b and 35, Jesus said:

*"For the mouth speaks what the heart is full of. A good man brings good things out of the good stored up in him, and an evil man brings evil things out of the evil stored up in him".*

This is why every time someone believes, the words that come from the mouth will be according to that belief.

Words produce actions, as the tongue is like the rudder in a ship, according to James 3:4 and 5:

*"Or take ships as an example. Although they are so large and are driven by strong winds, they are steered by a very small rudder wherever the pilot wants to go. Likewise, the tongue is a small part of the body, but it makes great boasts. Consider what a great forest is set on fire by a small spark".*

Our destiny is shaped by the words we say and confess. Negative words produce negative results and positive words produce positive results.

In 2 Corinthians 4:13, we read:

*"It is written: "I believed; therefore I have spoken." Since we have that same spirit of faith, we also believe and therefore speak".*

When we believe, we have the spirit of faith, and therefore we speak, which means that the words that come out of our mouths will be according to what we believe.

In Mark 11:23, Jesus declared:

*"Truly I tell you, if anyone **says** to this mountain, 'Go, throw yourself into the sea,' and does not doubt in their heart but believes that what they **say** will happen, it will be done for them."*

Jesus is stating that the person that believes will declare with their mouth that whatever she/he **says** is going to happen.

What Jesus is saying is that belief is the most important, but it requires words that back up the belief, like a seal. It is not just staying in front of the mountain, thinking that it will move... it won't move by your thoughts, but by your words!

What words are coming out of your mouth? Are they displaying what you believe? I've learned that, if I just open my mouth to say what is before my eyes, there are not going to be any changes.

If I just say: "Man, look at the size of the mountain that is in front of me", or "How in the world is this huge mountain going to be removed and thrown into the sea?" or even say: "I give up! There is nothing I can do to resolve this huge mess in my life". I understand that the mountain is not a little hill and that the situation is really challenging, but if you keep saying and repeating these words, not only the mountain won't be moved, but the situation will become worse since you will be discouraged and convinced by the temporary reality you are facing in front of you. This is exactly when a decision must be made. Either you keep on confessing the words of defeat or confess what the word of God says about it.

The word of God is eternal. Jesus declared, in Matthew 24:35:

*"Heaven and earth will pass away, but my words will never pass away".*

Every situation in the world is temporary, and the word of God is eternal, this means that any temporary and transitional situation can be changed and conformed to the eternal and immutable word of God.

Let me illustrate it: Suppose a person becomes sick today. This means that yesterday she or he was healthy, so tomorrow can be healed and okay again. This just shows how temporary circumstances are movable and changeable and eternal is unmovable and unchangeable.

As an example, I will mention the woman with the bleeding disorder, as it is written in Mark 5:25 to 34:

*And a woman was there who had suffered from bleeding for twelve years. She had borne much agony under the care of many physicians and had spent all she had, but to no avail. Instead, her condition had only grown worse. When the woman heard about Jesus, she came up through the crowd behind Him and touched His cloak. **For she kept saying,** "If only I touch His* *garments, I will be healed." Immediately her bleeding stopped, and she sensed in her body that she was healed of her affliction. At once Jesus was aware that power had gone out from Him. Turning to the crowd, He asked, "Who touched My garments?" His disciples answered, "You can see the crowd pressing in on You, and yet You ask, 'Who touched Me?'" But He kept looking around to see who had done this. Then the woman, knowing what had happened to her, came and fell down before Him trembling in fear, and she told Him the whole truth. "Daughter," said Jesus, "your faith has healed you. Go in peace and be free of your affliction."*

It is interesting that the word that denotes she kept "saying" is *Legó*, in the original, which means: to say (speak), moving it to a conclusion.

She was declaring what she had in her heart and received what she believed in.

What words are you expressing? Are they breaking the shell of the seed of faith? Great! If not, it is time for you to start believing in your heart and confessing with your mouth the words according to what God has said about it.

When your words are aligned with the word of God, you are declaring that what is eternal and immutable will act and transform what is mutable and temporary.

FAITH WORKS!!!

## SUGGESTED PRAYER *(say it out loud, if possible)*:

I take total and absolute control and responsibility over my spirit, soul, and body and totally break and cancel in the spiritual realm all the words I've said and the negative confession I've made, contrary to what the word of God declares. I now align my mouth and the words that come out of my mouth to be precisely according to what God declared. I now believe and declare that all my temporary circumstances will be transformed by the eternal, unchangeable, and immutable word of God. God is faithful and powerful enough to make what is circumstantial and changeable into the reality of His word, which is eternal, in Jesus' name, amen!

# CHAPTER 14

# PROCRASTINATION
## (Systematic postponing)

P rocrastination is the decision to postpone something important that could and should be done now.

Our brain liberates Dopamine[2], bringing a feeling of pleasure when we postpone something, due to the relief we feel for not having the obligation of deciding immediately, but this is tricky and can create a pattern of procrastination.

There is an occasional postponing when the person decides that making a decision right now would require too much of her/him, or it is not the proper time, yet, but there is a systematic postponing that indicates that procrastination is been established as a behavioral pattern, which displays insecurity and fear in most of the cases.

When facing a "fight or flight" situation, the procrastinator always chooses the flight, trying to avoid the stress of having to make a decision and sometimes the fear of the unknown that the decision will make her/him have to face.

Always procrastinating on important decisions can make people miss a lot, if not all that she/he could achieve, and fulfill that purpose for what she/he was born to fulfill, creating a void and frustration along with the feeling that there is always something missing.

Did you ever lay down your head on the pillow and started asking yourself:

*"Is it all I should be doing?"*;

*"I feel that something is missing in my life"*;

*"It doesn't matter how much I achieve and move forward in life, this void inside of me is like a thirst that can't be quenched"*;

*"I am trying to fulfill my inner frustration with things that are detrimental and dangerous, but I am just not able to stop by myself"*;

*"I am gaining weight by directing all my satisfaction to eat, and it became compulsive, but still the frustration is there"*;

*"I've gone through the process of changing how I look, but I am still not satisfied."*

This list is not comprehensive, which means that we could go on and on with all the thoughts people have that neglect the most important: no real satisfaction can be achieved unless the decision is made to fulfill the purpose why she/he has been born to fulfill.

This decision can't be procrastinated indefinitely, since it can put your life in danger of depression, desperation, anxiety, anguish, and the desire to just give it all up and ultimately end your life.

There is not something more fulfilling that brings more satisfaction than being useful and helping someone else.

Jesus declared in John 15:16:

> *"You did not choose me, but I chose you and appointed you **so that you might go and bear fruit** — **fruit that will last** — and so that whatever you ask in my name the Father will give you".*

There is no tree that benefits from the fruits it produces. This means that the orange tree doesn't benefit from the oranges it produces; the apple tree doesn't eat apples, and so on and so forth.

I've never seen a tree requesting applause and recognition for the fruits it is producing to keep on producing. We just approach it, get the fruit, and leave.

You were born to be fruitful. When you start being a blessing to someone or even to several people, Oxytocin, which is a hormone that produces satisfaction will be released, and you will understand why the bible teaches us in Acts 20:35:

*"In everything I did, I showed you that by this kind of hard work, we must help the weak, remembering the words the Lord Jesus himself said: 'It is more blessed to give than to receive.'"*

More blessed it is to give than to receive means that there is a tremendous need all around us crying out for help, even among people who look like their life is great and display a happy life. Smiles can be deceiving, so people are going through rough times, even when they are displaying a nice face, being courteous, and smiling.

So much need in the world, mainly after the pandemic of 2020, which shook up all the ground people were relying upon.

When are you going to stop procrastinating and make the decision to move forward and achieve everything you are suppose to achieve?

Let me give you an example:

My wife and I have always been very supportive and dedicated to our children. We have 2 boys and a girl. They are grown up now.

Since we have always been so united and have had the opportunity to provide a very healthy and nice childhood to them, it created a bond between us that was wonderful.

My wife and I have spent all our childhood in Brazil, where the culture is overly protective of kids and hiring a maid is not very expensive, mainly to the upper-middle class, which was both our cases.

This means that the maid is the one who does most of the work in the house, and not just the chores, but cooking, cleaning, etc.

My parents emancipated me at an early age, and my father had an attitude of support, but let me face the challenges of life on my own, which was good, but very painful, so it created in me the desire to, in the future, protect my own children from the reality, toughness, and difficulties of life.

Before moving to the US, we lived in a big property, we had 3 maids, so our kids were not used to doing chores or anything else in the house, just like when we were kids.

When we came to the US, we faced the opposite situation, since having a maid is very expensive and the kids are supposed to have responsibilities starting at a young age even in the por upper-middle class of society, which is very good.

So, remembering my own experience at a young age, I've developed an overprotective behavior that tried everything possible to avoid frustrations and deceptions to my kids.

The Lord started dealing with me about this in 1999 when I was confronted by a friend, so I made some progress but didn't change my overprotective behavior as I should.

I have procrastinated the emancipation of my kids for years and years, not admitting to myself that they had to face their own problems and had to decide on their own what, when, and how to face the challenges and obstacles in life and make their own decisions.

The Lord has tried to deal with me in that regard, but I loved to be asked by my kids for counsel and direction and would even feel offended if they just decided and moved forward in life on their own, even after leaving our home and getting married or living by themselves.

I know that I should change, but for some reason, always procrastinated that decision. Even in some situations that were designed and put together by God to mature my kids and to make them stronger, I made all the effort to help somehow, even when I was not in a situation, or with the proper conditions to help.

Some years ago, I understood that this was not just detrimental to me but was also keeping them from growing and facing the situations and challenges they were responsible to face to mature.

I had to repent and ask the Lord for forgiveness, so since then, I only help my kids if, and when they ask for my counsel, and I respect them on the decisions they make.

This was a shell in my faith in that area it was hard to see a breakthrough, but it worked and released me to believe that the Lord is taking care of my kids, and His will is the best for them.

If you are procrastinating a decision that must be made, you are just postponing something that you will have to do. This procrastination only enforces and strengthens the shell of faith and keeps it from germinating and producing.

Make the decision to stop procrastinating and break free of the shell of the seed of faith now! Move forward and achieve the goals and fulfill the purpose you were born to fulfill!

FAITH WORKS!!!

## SUGGESTED PRAYER *(say it out loud, if possible)*:

I now take full and absolute authority and responsibility over my spirit, soul, and body and decide that every decision I must make won't be postponed anymore. I will have all the courage, strength, and boldness necessary to make all the right decisions and stand by them. I rebuke all and every thought, argument, and excuse to procrastinate. The Spirit God gave me does not make me timid, but gives me power, love, and self-discipline, according to II Timothy 1:7.

I trust in the will of God to my life and His expectation that I should make the proper decisions about them, which I now make to obey my Lord and Savior, in Jesus' name, amen.

# CHAPTER 15

# CIRCUMSTANCES (Convinced by the environment)

We are highly bombarded by all kinds of information, mainly audio and visual through social media, TV, newspapers, billboards, our environment, etc., that can affect our thoughts and emotions all the time.

We can't ignore them, but we can choose to keep believing, despite our circumstances being contrary to what we are believing.

So many times, I've witnessed in my life and in the lives of other people the situation becoming worse after they started believing and declaring victory over it.

It is like the environment is trying to convince us that victory is not going to be achieved and the miracle is not going to happen.

This is the shell of the seed that can either be broken or strengthened, depending on our position and decision.

When we decide to believe what the word of God says about the situation, the shell is going to be broken, and the DNA of faith is going to be released, and the supernatural is going to operate and work in the situation, changing it in our favor.

God has all the power to do and perform what He has promised, and immeasurably more, according to Ephesians 3:20 and 21:

> *"Now to him who is able to do immeasurably more than all we ask or imagine, **according to his power that is at work within us**, to him be glory in the church and in Christ Jesus throughout all generations, for ever and ever! Amen".*

Notice that the problem is not God's ability or strength to perform, but how His power is working within us.

I've mentioned before that God has established how His power and operation are going to be released and effective, which is through faith. He doesn't move because there is a need. He has established a way that our needs will be fulfilled: through faith and His power that works within us.

Even the wrath of man does not produce the righteousness of God, according to James 1:19 and 20:

> *"My dear brothers and sisters, take note of this: Everyone should be quick to listen, slow to speak and*

*slow to become angry, because **human anger does not produce the righteousness that God desires***.

If the circumstances are trying to convince you differently about what God has said, choose to believe that what He has promised will be done; break the shell of what you see and hear, and make the decision to believe that He who has promised is able to perform it.

For the first example, I want to share a very powerful and interesting situation that David has gone through.

It is recorded in I Samuel chapters 29 and 30.

David and his men were out of their town Ziklag, with the army of Achish, and they were sent back home, which was 3 days away from where they were camping.

When they arrived at Ziklag, they found out that the Amalekites had attacked, burned it, and taken all their wives and children captive.

When David and his men saw that situation, they wept so much, and so loud, until they had no strength left to weep, and David was greatly distressed because the men were talking of stoning him; each one was bitter in spirit because of their sons and daughters.

But David found strength in the LORD his God. (Verse 6)

Just imagine the circumstance: the whole situation was conspiring against David, but he found strength in the Lord his God. This strength is only achieved through faith. He decided to break the shell of faith, not allowing the circumstances to convince him that there was no solution to the situation.

Because of his decision and position, he went with his men after the Amalekites, according to the revelation God gave to him, fought, and overcame their army, took every single life, including all the wives and children back, and on the top of it, all the plunders, which were so much, that he divided with several people that were in 14 different cities.

Defeat into victory: God gave the strength, the favor, and the courage to David to turn a situation that was desperate, and looking impossible into a blessing and a victory even better than it was before, with reaches and plunder.

Faith works!!!

Another example in my own life in the first quarter of 2023:

After I left my job, I was praying and looking for a position, but the situation was not easy, and my financial reserves were getting depleted. In talking to my wife, we were becoming really concerned about the situation, after weeks had passed by with no results.

I was surrounded by bad news from the companies I was applying to, but I just decided to break the shell of the seed of faith and believe in the word of God, which declares, in Philippians 4:19:

*"And my God will meet all your needs according to the riches of his glory in Christ Jesus".*

Just as I started declaring this verse and some others about this situation, on a Wednesday morning, while I was doing my devotional, the Lord reminded me of an encounter I had with a businessman 1 day after I left that job, so I called him, and he expressed that he needed my services at his company. I've started working there and getting much more than the amount I was getting in the job I had before, enabling me to recover all that was spent and have a surplus.

Faith works!!!

I don't know how hard and challenging your situation is, but it is hardly like the situation that Job faced, where he lost all his properties, children, and even health, but he decided to break the shell of the seed, by repenting (Job 42:6) and praying for his friends, who were criticizing, and accusing him (Job 42:10). The Lord just turned his situation around, even giving him twice what he had before, restoring his health, his life, and all the goods and properties back, in such an abundance, that even his female daughters, who were the most beautiful in all the land, got an inheritance along with their brothers.

Decide now to break the shell of faith, by stopping believing in the circumstances and believing that God is going to turn things around, and move in such a way, that your miracle is going to happen, and the victory is going to be achieved.

## SUGGESTED PRAYER *(say it out loud, if possible)*:

I now take full and absolute authority and responsibility over my spirit, soul, and body, and decide to believe and acknowledge that the word of God is eternal and immutable, and my circumstances are temporary and mutable, so I now declare and command my circumstances to be changed, adjusted, and aligned to the word of God. I rebuke, cast out, and order all the evil activity, and darkness in my life and circumstances to get out never to come back. I stand in the authority of the name of Jesus and fulfill what my master Jesus Christ has declared, which is that I will "trample on snakes and scorpions and overcome all the power of the enemy; nothing will harm me". Jesus has overcome the devil, overpowering him, took away all his power and armor, and divided up his plunder. Jesus has all the authority in heaven and on earth and his name is above all the names, so it is in His name that I move and live, doing everything in obedience and humbleness, because "God opposes the proud but shows favor to the humble."

Thank you, Father, for doing everything for my good, because I love you, and have been called according to Your purpose, in Jesus' name, amen.

# CHAPTER 16

# PRIORITIES (Purpose/vision)

Now, that you know how to break the shell of the seed of faith, it is important to put your life in perspective and have a broader understanding and vision of why you were born.

What is the most important question anyone should ask and seek the answer with all their heart? It is:

"Why am I here, what is the reason that I was born, is there a purpose, a vision for my life, and am I fulfilling it?"

Seeking answers to these questions, made me establish only ONE goal in my life, which is to listen to the phrase spoken by my Lord Jesus Christ:

> *"Come, you who are blessed by my Father; take your inheritance, the kingdom prepared for you since the creation of the world". Matthew 25:34*

Everything I do or avoid doing is directly connected with this goal.

There are only 2 phrases that will be spoken by Jesus on the judgment day: the one I've mentioned above, and this one:

> *"Depart from me, you who are cursed, into the eternal fire prepared for the devil and his angels".* *Matthew 25:41.*

Everyone should be totally and absolutely committed to doing everything possible to avoid hearing this second phrase. It means that the person will be damned for all eternity. It is not 80 or 90 years; **it is forever and ever!!!**

When we understand the reason why we were born, it makes us establish priorities, because they will make us reach the goal or miss it.

Everyone that was born in the world is here for a purpose. No one was just born by chance or coincidence. Even the ones that were born out of rape or by an act of irresponsibility of two teenagers were born to fulfill a purpose, a vision.

What is the vision? It is the purpose of God's heart revealed to people for the fulfillment of a goal, a target, an objective preset by God before the foundation of the world.

Let me give you an illustration of the difference between a broad vision and a narrow one:

When you come very close to see a large painting, like only 2 or 3 inches from it, you will only see a little portion, and miss the whole picture. You will make your opinion and conclusion with very few points, according to your observation, and miss the beauty of the painting which, if you take five or more steps back, you are going to be able to see and admire in its entirety.

It is so easy to go through the motions in life, doing what most people are doing, like growing up, marrying someone, having kids, getting old, and dying. Is that it?

I mentioned in an earlier chapter that Jesus commended us to be fruitful. I also mentioned that no tree is benefited by the fruits it produces; it always benefits someone other than the tree that produced it. The tree is never looking for recognition, awards, or applauses, but staying still and producing fruits at the proper season.

When we die, the Lord is not going to ask how much money we've made, which sports team we cheered for, or even if we had a religion, or have attended church meetings faithfully.

In Revelation 22:12, the Lord declares:

> *"Look, I am coming soon! My reward is with me, and I will give to each person according to what they have done".*

It is not just by what we did in terms of activities, but by whether and how we have fulfilled or not the purpose for what we were born.

Everything we do, either good or bad, makes a ripple effect, influencing people all around us and, according to neuroscience recent discoveries, will affect even our DNA[3], which means, the next generations.

What is the legacy you intend to leave, not just to your children and grandchildren, but to humanity? It doesn't mean that you must do something big, to impact millions, but if you fulfill the purpose you were born to fulfill, you will impact positively the people you get in contact with, and they will also impact others positively, and so on.

There is a movie by Disney that shows how deviating from the vision can lead to frustration and unfulfilled results. It is called: The Kid[4]. It is interesting to watch how and why the main character had the course of his life changed by a trauma created when he was only 8 years old.

The most fulfilling experience a person can have is to fulfill the purpose for what he/she was born to fulfill. When the person isn't fulfilling it, everything that he/she tries to fill that gap with, won't work.

Let me give you an example of someone who didn't follow the vision:

I know about a lady who, since an early age, she dreamed of going to Africa to help the poor and teach the kids, but when she started dating who now is her husband, she shared her vision with him, and he just said that they should consider it and think about it after they got married since this was not his vision at that point. They've got married and never went to Africa and she is frustrated all this time. God can use her, and she can be a blessing in another way, but she is always going to be dreaming and wondering about the mission in Africa and how much she could be doing down there.

In another example, I would like to use the life of someone who has fulfilled the vision:

Pr. Billy Graham, one of the most important Americans of all time: He was a preacher all his life and the counselor for Presidents and dignitaries. The ripple effect this has produced is impressive: millions upon millions of people received the Lord Jesus as their personal savior all over the world, he had a TV broadcast that has reached and still blesses billions, daily devotions, 34 books published, preached in 185 countries, thousands were blessed, reached, and helped by the ministry he has established, called Billy Graham Evangelistic Association, through several services, ministries, and actions it provides to help in catastrophes, feeding the hungry in several countries, etc., etc., etc. He could accept any position in a large corporation, or even become a politician, but he had only ONE goal in mind: fulfill the calling the Lord Jesus commanded him to fulfill until the end of his life, at age 99.

The legacy of this boy from Charlotte, North Carolina is impressive, and it clearly displays what happens when a person understands the vision and fulfills it.

It was by developing a daily devotional every morning that I was able to understand the vision and am fulfilling it in my life.

There is no way to receive and understand the vision, other than by developing a relationship with the Lord on a daily basis, since there are so many details and aspects that should be understood and implemented, mainly regarding: What, How, When, and Where the different parts of the vision must be completed.

The vision is challenging, and you will need faith, but also courage, boldness, wisdom, patience, and persistence to break all the obstacles and barriers that will appear in front of you, trying to make you quit.

Every single morning, I have the privilege of spending time with the Lord, and developing a priceless relationship. It is the most important part of my day. He is so awesome, wonderful, lovely, tremendous, merciful, powerful, righteous, magnificent, glorious, compassionate, radiant, etc., etc., etc. that I could spend the rest of my days in His majestic presence, just in awe of Him and who He is.

Jesus told us to develop this relationship in Matthew 6:6:

> "But when you pray, go into your room, close the door and pray to your Father, who is unseen. Then your Father, who sees what is done in secret, will reward you".

Jesus is talking about a special time, and place where we develop intimacy with the Father. There are some things that I've learned to practice that are fundamental to developing this relationship:

Since I know that my soul has the tendency to become worried and anxious before I check messages and social media, and get worried, anxious, and distracted by news and events, I shut down my door, not just physically, but also subjectively, dividing the "outside" from the "inside". Outside is everything about life and inside it is only me and my heavenly father. I am isolating myself from all the issues, chaos, activism, opinions of others, winds of doctrine, the turbulence of life, stress, gossiping, the world, news, waves of influence, turmoil, rush, etc., etc., etc.

In Psalm 131:2, it is written:

*"But I have calmed and quieted my soul, like a weaned child with its mother; like a weaned child is my soul within me".*

Calming and quieting our soul is the most challenging act since our soul is like a child "thirsty for milk". Our soul demands immediate answers, positions, and decisions, so calming and quieting it down is something that sometimes requires time and persistence. When we calm down our soul, we can enter and enjoy fellowship between our spirit, and our Father. It is then, that we reach another dimension, the spiritual realm, and receive peace, joy, freedom, forgiveness, love, wisdom, discernment, courage, boldness, understanding, identity, compassion, goodness, mercy, miracles, strength, energy, abundant life, sonship, godliness, meekness, self-control, and all the riches and radiance of His glory.

Make the priority in your daily routine to wake up earlier to spend time with the Lord in prayer, meditation in the Bible, adoration, and praise and you will start to experience the most exhilarating feeling: the presence of God!

## SUGGESTED PRAYER *(say it out loud, if possible)*:

I now take full and absolute authority and responsibility over my spirit, soul, and body and decide to set up my priorities according to God's will and plan for my life. I agree with the word of God which says that I should seek first the kingdom of God and all other things shall be added to my life. I don't prioritize material things in my existence. I acknowledge that I was born to fulfill the purpose of God's heart for my life and consecrate myself to accomplish all the goals and results that will glorify my master Jesus Christ.

I establish as the most important target of my life to align my actions and words to hear my dear savior saying on that glorious day: *"Come, you who are blessed by my Father; take your inheritance, the kingdom prepared for you since the creation of the world"*.

In Jesus' name, amen!

# CONCLUSION

Faith is so wonderful and powerful that I can't even imagine how my life would be without it. It is the very core of my existence and life.

I've shared in this book just a few examples of what happens when we break the shell of the seed of faith, but could mention many, many more since it is a lifestyle that I've decided to live upon.

I can only say that God is wonderful and faithful, and giving my life to Him was the best and most important decision I've ever made!

Jesus' accomplishments, and victories are available to you and anyone who believes and accepts Him, according to John 1:12. All you must do is repent of your sins, open your heart and mouth, and confess Jesus Christ as your Lord and Savior. If you've never done it, you can do it now! Just pray out loud, telling Him that you believe that Jesus has died to pay for your sins, that you repent for your sins and for living your life on your own terms and lordship, you accept Him in your life now, renouncing all the other lords you've had, ask his forgiveness, and declare Him the Lord of your life until the end, in Jesus' name, Amen!

He is worthy of all the glory and all the praise... the work Jesus did is tremendous, and He deserves all the glory, praise, majesty, honor, thanksgiving, exaltation, adoration, respect, dedication, consecration, and trust forever and ever! Amen!

God is fulfilling what He promised in the book of Joel 2:28-32, which promises an outpouring of the Holy Spirit. We have seen around the world an awakening and revival taking place in various countries and locations.

Your faith will be very important for this great revival to be effective and reach many, many people to be saved, transformed, and healed. Do not allow the advance of immoral and harmful practices that have been spread around the world to strengthen the shell of faith but decide to break it and shine in the midst of this corrupted and wicked generation, as the light of the world and salt of the earth, which is what Jesus called you to be. May the light of Christ shine through your life, reflecting like a mirror the glory of God! God bless you!

FAITH WORKS!!!!!

# BIBLIOGRAPHY

1. Neuroplasticity: https://www.psychologytoday. com/us/basics/neuroplasticity

2. Procrastination: <u>Timothy A. Pychyl</u>, PhD, a psychology professor at Carleton University, in Ottawa, and the author of *The Procrastinator's Digest: A Concise Guide to Solving the Procrastination Puzzle.*

3. Our DNA: www.scientificamerican.com/ article/early-life-experience-its-in-your-dna/

4. Movie: The Kid, 2000. Stars: Bruce Willis, Spencer Breslin, Emily Mortimer

# ABOUT THE AUTHOR

Born and raised in an evangelical home, Helio Vassão Nespoli had his real experience of conversion in 1974, when he was 15 years old. He married Silvia Nespoli in 1982 and they have 3 grown up kids. He felt a calling to preach and be a minister of the gospel since his conversion, was ordained a pastor in 1985, and started planting churches with his wife, who was ordained in 1997. Together, they've planted 7 churches both in the US and Brazil. They have been ministering in over 100 churches during their ministry. They were appointed counselors at EIFOL (an associated ministry of YWAM – Youth with a Mission). They have counseled individually hundreds of people in the courses as well as in the churches they were invited to minister. He has a Bachelor, Master, and Doctorate degrees from the former Florida Theological Seminary (now called Florida Christian University). Dr. Nespoli also has a calling for business and has worked from 1981 through 1997 as an animal dentist both in Brazil and the USA and was a licensed Business Broker in the State of Florida, selling companies from owners of diverse cultural backgrounds to buyers of different cultures and languages. In 1999 he was invited to be the Vice President of the American company responsible for bringing the Endowment Fund of Harvard University along with the Prudential insurance company to invest in Brazil, among other institutional investors.

Throughout his life, Dr. Nespoli has exercised and lived by faith. After understanding how faith works, which is explained in this book, he was able to fulfill the calling of God to his life, which is to help people achieve their full potential in God and accomplish the purpose of why they were born.

This book is not just theory, but the expression of a reality the author has practiced and the victories he was able to achieve against all the shells of the seed of faith, enabling it to be released and bear fruits for the glory of God.

**FAITH WORKS!!!**

Made in the USA
Monee, IL
17 October 2023